Liberating
love

EXODUS

by Tim Chester

Exodus For You

If you are reading *Exodus For You* alongside this Good Book Guide, here is how the studies in this booklet link to the chapters of *Exodus For You*:

Study One → Ch 1   Study Five → Ch 7-8
Study Two → Ch 2-3   Study Six → Ch 8-10
Study Three → Ch 4-5   Study Seven → Ch 13-14
Study Four → Ch 6   Study Eight → Ch 11-12, 15

Find out more about *Exodus For You* at:
www.thegoodbook.com/for-you

Liberating love
The Good Book Guide to Exodus
© Tim Chester/The Good Book Company, 2016. Reprinted 2019, 2020, 2023.
Series Consultants: Tim Chester, Tim Thornborough,
                    Anne Woodcock, Carl Laferton

the good book
COMPANY

thegoodbook.com | thegoodbook.co.uk
thegoodbook.com.au | thegoodbook.co.nz | thegoodbook.co.in

Unless indicated, all Scripture references are taken from the Holy Bible, New International Version. Copyright © 2011 Biblica, Inc. Used by permission.

Tim Chester has asserted his right under the Copyright, Designs and Patents Act 1988 to be identified as author of this work.

ISBN: 9781784980269 | Printed in India

CONTENTS

Introduction   4
Why study Exodus?   5

1. People with a promise   7
   Exodus 1 – 2

2. When God gets involved   13
   Exodus 3 – 6

3. God v Pharaoh   19
   Exodus 7 – 13

4. Through the sea   25
   Exodus 13 v 17 – 15 v 21

5. Trouble on the road   31
   Exodus 15 v 22 – 18 v 27

6. You shall...   39
   Exodus 19 – 24

7. The golden calf: tragedy and mercy   47
   Exodus 32 – 34

8. At home with God   55
   Exodus 25 – 31; 35 – 40

Leader's Guide   62

Introduction: Good Book Guides

Every Bible-study group is different—yours may take place in a church building, in a home or in a cafe, on a train, over a leisurely mid-morning coffee or squashed into a 30-minute lunch break. Your group may include new Christians, mature Christians, non-Christians, mums and tots, students, businessmen or teens. That's why we've designed these *Good Book Guides* to be flexible for use in many different situations.

Our aim in each session is to uncover the meaning of a passage, and see how it fits into the "big picture" of the Bible. But that can never be the end. We also need to appropriately apply what we have discovered to our lives. Let's take a look at what is included:

⊕ **Talkabout:** Most groups need to "break the ice" at the beginning of a session, and here's the question that will do that. It's designed to get people talking around a subject that will be covered in the course of the Bible study.

⊕ **Investigate:** The Bible text for each session is broken up into manageable chunks, with questions that aim to help you understand what the passage is about. The **Leader's Guide** contains **guidance for questions**, and sometimes ☑ additional "follow-up" questions.

⊙ **Explore more (optional):** These questions will help you connect what you have learned to other parts of the Bible, so you can begin to fit it all together like a jig-saw; or occasionally look at a part of the passage that's not dealt with in detail in the main study.

→ **Apply:** As you go through a Bible study, you'll keep coming across **apply** sections. These are questions to get the group discussing what the Bible teaching means in practice for you and your church. ⊡ **Getting personal** is an opportunity for you to think, plan and pray about the changes that you personally may need to make as a result of what you have learned.

↑ **Pray:** We want to encourage prayer that is rooted in God's word—in line with his concerns, purposes and promises. So each session ends with an opportunity to review the truths and challenges highlighted by the Bible study, and turn them into prayers of request and thanksgiving.

The **Leader's Guide** and introduction provide historical background information, explanations of the Bible texts for each session, ideas for **optional extra** activities, and guidance on how best to help people uncover the truths of God's word.

Why study Exodus?

A princess goes to bathe in the river, and has her heart won by the cries of an abandoned baby.

A bush on fire never burns up, and from it speaks a voice that will change history.

An unarmed shepherd walks out of the wilderness to do battle with the most powerful man on earth.

The lone cry of a bereaved mother is joined by another, and then another, and then another, until a loud wailing echoes across the land.

A whole nation walks through a sea, with walls of water on either side, to liberation on the far shore.

Amid thunder, lightning, thick cloud and an earthquake, the voice of God booms across a plain.

In the wilderness, a man argues with God about the future of a people, and God relents.

The glory of God so fills a tent that everyone must evacuate.

There is no shortage of dramatic moments in the book of Exodus. It is a story that has repeatedly captured the public imagination and which has been a favourite of film-makers. But in truth, its message is more dramatic than these dramatic moments and more revolutionary than these revolutionary movements.

The book of Exodus is not simply an inspiring tale from the past. It is our story. The Old Testament prophets promised a new exodus: a repeat of the exodus that would be more dramatic and more revolutionary. The exodus sets God's story on a trajectory that comes to a climax with the life, death and resurrection of Jesus. The book of Exodus is absolutely key to understanding the person and work of Jesus, and appreciating the liberating love that brought him into this world and took him to the cross.

These eight studies will take you through Exodus, showing you God, thrilling you about being a member of his people, and challenging you to live in joyful awe of him. Exodus is an exciting story. It is a historical story. And, as it points us to and inspires us to worship Christ, it is our story.

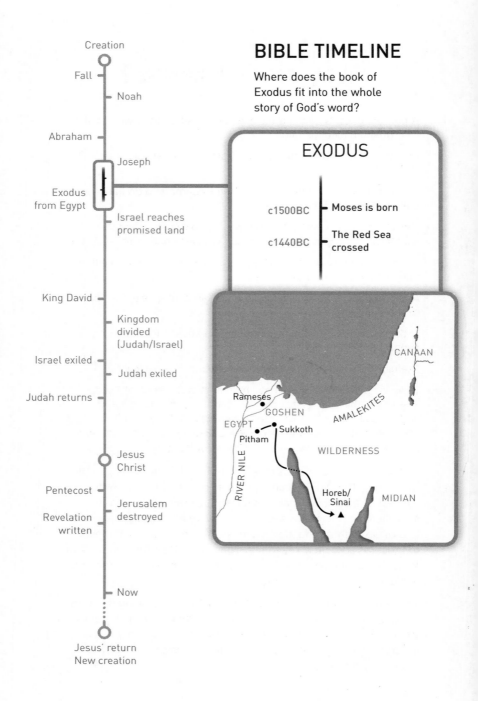

BIBLE TIMELINE

Where does the book of Exodus fit into the whole story of God's word?

Creation
Fall
Noah
Abraham
Joseph
Exodus from Egypt
Israel reaches promised land

King David
Kingdom divided (Judah/Israel)
Israel exiled
Judah exiled
Judah returns

Jesus Christ
Pentecost
Jerusalem destroyed
Revelation written

Now

Jesus' return
New creation

EXODUS

c1500BC — Moses is born

c1440BC — The Red Sea crossed

CANAAN
Rameses
GOSHEN
AMALEKITES
EGYPT
Pitham
Sukkoth
RIVER NILE
WILDERNESS
Horeb/Sinai
MIDIAN

1

Exodus 1 – 2
PEOPLE WITH A PROMISE

⊕ **talkabout**

1. Have you ever relied on someone's promise to you? What was it about them that made you trust them? Did you ever worry that they might not keep it?

⊕ **investigate**

❯ **Read Exodus 1 v 1-7**

In the original Hebrew, the book of Exodus actually begins with the word "and". It immediately alerts us to the fact that this story is part of a bigger story…

2. **Read Genesis 12 v 1-7; 15 v 1-21; 17 v 15-22.** What did God promise, and to whom?

Abraham's son was Isaac, and his son was Jacob, which brings us to Exodus 1 v 1.

3. How is God keeping his promise in Exodus 1 v 1-7?

▶ Read Exodus 1 v 8-21

4. How is God's promise-keeping threatened in these verses?

• In what ways is Pharaoh's plan thwarted?

▶ Read Exodus 1 v 22 – 2 v 10

5. How does Pharaoh raise the stakes (1 v 22)? What is ironic about the way in which his plans are thwarted (2 v 1-10)?

⊡ **explore more**

optional

Israel's fruitfulness here shows God is keeping his promise to Abraham.

▶ Read Genesis 1 v 26-29

How is it also a mark of Israel keeping God's command to all humanity?

▶ Read Genesis 3 v 8-15

What had God promised would be the relationship between the snake and the woman (v 15)?
How are Pharaoh's actions in Exodus 1 a fulfilment of the promise of Genesis 3 v 15?

So Egypt will be the site of the ongoing battle between those who belong to the snake, and those who belong to the promise.

What significance does this add to the coming showdown between God and Pharaoh?

⊟ apply

6. What does Exodus 1 teach us about the promise-keeping of God? And the plans of powerful regimes?

• How should this encourage us as God's people today?

⊡ getting personal

Do you trust more in God to keep to his plans… or deep down, do you think that the plans of those who oppose him or his people are more likely to succeed? When are you most likely to act as though God will not come through for you?

Jesus promises, "I will build my church, and the gates of Hades will not overcome it" (Matthew 16 v 18). When do you most need to remember this verse?

⊡ investigate

This baby, Moses, now being raised as a Hebrew but with all the privileges of Egypt, will be the Hebrews' great liberator.

▶ Read Exodus 2 v 11-25

7. How are Moses' actions in verses 11-12 more "Egyptian" than godly? How do they undermine his ability to lead Israel (v 14-15)?

> **DICTIONARY**
>
> **Midian (v 15):** see next page.
> **Covenant (v 24):** binding agreement.

Moses ends up living as a Midianite. The Midianites were nomads, but they wandered all over the Sinai Peninsula and the land of Canaan—all areas of land promised to Abraham. And in Midian, in contrast to Egypt, the Lord was worshipped freely (the reference to a "priest" in verse 16 raises this possibility; 18 v 9-12 confirms it).

8. So in what sense has Moses left home, and in what sense has he come home?

9. By the end of chapter 2, to what extent has God kept his promises? What remains to be fulfilled?

    • How do verses 23-25 suggest that God is about to intervene in Israelite history?

10. **Read Hebrews 11 v 24-27.** Why did Moses choose to live as an Israelite, rather than an Egyptian? What did he give up in order to do so?

11. **Re-read Exodus 1 v 15-18.** Why did Shiphrah and Puah not obey Pharaoh? What were they risking in order to disobey him?

→ **apply**

12. How do you face similar choices to Moses, and to Shiphrah and Puah? What would it look like for you to choose to fear God and live by faith, as they did?

⊡ **getting personal**

Are there ways in which you fear people more than God? What would change if you trusted in his promises rather than being swayed by human plans? How will you remember to fear and trust God?

↑ **pray**

Thank God that he is both a promise-making and a promise-keeping God. Thank him for the confidence and assurance that can give you as you walk through life.

Pray together about the times when you must choose between fearing God or fearing man, based on your answers to Question Twelve.

2 Exodus 3 – 6
WHEN GOD GETS INVOLVED

The story so far

The Israelites are numerous, but enslaved and killed by Pharaoh in Egypt. One baby, Moses, is rescued from death, and, as an adult, flees to Midian.

⊕ talkabout

1. What's the hardest thing you've ever been asked to do?

⊥ investigate

> ❯ **Read Exodus 3 v 1-22**

2. Sum up the events of v 1-14 in a couple of sentences or a couple of pictures.

3. What does God promise in this meeting with Moses?
   • v 7-10, 17

   • v 12

- v 18

- v 19-22

4. What do we learn about who God is and what he is like?
- v 2

- v 5

- v 7

- v 12

- v 14 (use the footnote to help with this)

- v 15 (also v 6)

5. How will the character of God be revealed by the actions of God?

6. What is Moses' worry in verse 11? How is God's response in verse 12 both not an answer to Moses, and also the best answer to Moses?

getting personal

To what extent do you allow your identity—what gives you confidence and how you feel about yourself—to be founded on the truth that "I will be with you"? When is this hardest for you? How might remembering "I will be with you" help you in those times or circumstances?

⊡ apply

7. Read John 8 v 54-59. What is Jesus claiming about himself here?

• Look over your answers to question 4. This is who Jesus is. How similar or different is that to how you tend to describe him, individually and as a church?

8. What do you find hard in the Christian life? How does Moses and God's exchange in v 10-12 both comfort and challenge you?

⊡ investigate

▶ **Read Exodus 4 v 1-23**

DICTIONARY

Leprous (v 6): infected with leprosy, a skin disease.
Eloquent (v 10): good with words.

explore more

optional

What problems does Moses have with what God has asked him to do (v 1, 10, 13)?

What do God's responses show about himself, and about how he deals with his people?

Verses 24-26 relate a strange episode, which raises questions which we can't readily answer 3,000 years on. But bear in mind that God has just drawn a line between the firstborn of God and the firstborn of Egypt (v 22-23). The firstborn of Egypt will die because of Egypt's refusal to liberate the firstborn of God. So the line is stark—between grace and life, and judgment and death. And circumcision was the sign that someone was part of Israel, God's firstborn (Genesis 17). In not circumcising Gershom, Moses was treating him as an Egyptian, and not a member of God's people. God's attack anticipates his attack on Pharaoh and Egypt. The only hope is to cross the line, to enter God's people—which is what Zipporah does when she circumcises Gershom.

Today, baptism is the sign that you have crossed the line and are part of God's "firstborn son"—his people—united to his eternal Son, Jesus.

> **Read Exodus 5 v 1-23**

9. What difference does God becoming involved make to his people's lives?

DICTIONARY

Obnoxious (v 21): offensive.

> **Read Exodus 6 v 1-12**

10. What does God add to his promises in verses 2-8?

DICTIONARY

Yoke (v 6): harness for ploughing animals; burden.
Redeem (v 6): set free for a price.

- How do verses 6-8 show us what it means to be "redeemed"? How does this apply to God's people today?

11. How do the people respond, and why (v 9)? Do you think it's justified?

➡ apply

12. Why is it so hard to keep trusting God when life gets harder, not better, as we follow him?

- What does this passage tell us we need to do when we feel as though God has abandoned us or is not worth following?

- Why do we have even less excuse than the Israelites for not listening to God's promises?

⊡ getting personal

It's very easy to trust God when he gives us what we want. It's far harder to trust him when that requires missing out, or brings trouble. When that happens, lift your eyes to the cross. See God working to bring good from evil, and see his love and commitment to you in giving you his only Son. That will rearrange your affections, and spark your gratitude... even in the hard times.

What will you choose to do this week? Complain, or praise?

⬆ pray

Spend time praising God for who he is (look back at your answers to Question Four to help). Then praise Jesus, God's Son, for being the great "I AM".

Pray about ways in which life, for your group or for others in your church, has got harder because they are following Christ, asking God to give them the grace to praise and trust him rather than complaining.

3 Exodus 7 – 13
GOD V PHARAOH

The story so far

The Israelites are numerous, but enslaved and killed by Pharaoh in Egypt. One baby, Moses, is rescued from death, and, as an adult, flees to Midian.

God appears to Moses, reveals his name, and sends him to tell Pharaoh to let Israel go. Pharaoh refuses. It's now a contest between the LORD and the king.

⊕ talkabout

1. Of those that you can actively remember, what have been the two or three most important positive events in your life?

   • How often do you think about them? In what situations do you call them to mind, and how do they make you feel?

⬇ investigate

▶ **Read Exodus 6 v 28 – 7 v 13**

2. How has Pharaoh challenged God (5 v 1-2)? What has God promised about Pharaoh and his people (7 v 5)?

DICTIONARY

Divisions (7 v 4): groups of people.

The plagues are the answer to Pharaoh's question, and the means by which God keeps his promise.

3. Fill out the table below as you look at the first nine plagues.

PLAGUE	PASSAGE	IS A WARNING GIVEN?	HOW DOES THE EGYPTIAN COURT RESPOND?	IS ISRAEL PROTECTED?	WHAT ARE WE TOLD ABOUT PHARAOH'S HEART?
	7 v 14-24				
	7 v 25 – 8 v 15				
	8 v 16-19				
	8 v 20-32				
	9 v 1-7				
	9 v 8-12				
	9 v 13-35				
	10 v 1-20				
	10 v 21-29 (also 11 v 3)				

4. Who hardened Pharaoh's heart?

• What does this tell us about God's control of everything, and about people's responsibility for their response to him?

Pharaoh wasn't an atheist—he believed in many gods. But he did not believe he should have to listen to Israel's God. And Pharaoh did not mind Israel worshipping their God. But he took offence at the idea that the God of Israel might have a claim on him.

5. How are the plagues an answer to Pharaoh's way of thinking?

☐→ apply

6. How do the plagues motivate and equip us to talk to friends who are happy for us to believe in "the Christian God", but don't believe they need to?

⊡ getting personal

Who do you know who has this kind of mindset? Might the LORD be prompting you to speak to them, gently but firmly, about him? Why not commit to praying each day for an opportunity to speak with them, the courage to take it, and the right words to say?

⊡ explore more

Shortly after the day of Pentecost, Peter and John heal a lame man outside the Jerusalem Temple. As a result, they are arrested, imprisoned and then brought before the Jewish Council. The question they are asked is, "By what power or what name did you do this?" (Acts 4 v 7). What authority? What name? It's an echo of Pharaoh's question, "Who is the Lord, that I should obey him?"

❯ Read Acts 4 v 8-22; Exodus 9 v 14, 16

What are the similarities between the purposes of the plagues and the purpose of the death and resurrection of Jesus Christ (Acts 4 v 10-12)?

What is one indicator that someone understands the authority Jesus has (v 13, 18-20)?

⊡ investigate

❯ Read Exodus 11 v 1 – 12 v 39

7. Which families face death, and why? Which families escape death, and how?

> **DICTIONARY**
>
> **Ordinance (12 v 14):** rule.
> **Sacred (v 16):** holy; dedicated to God.
> **Unleavened bread (v 17):** bread made without yeast.
> **Hyssop (v 22):** a type of wild shrub or plant.

• In what sense was there "not a house without someone dead" (v 30)?

8. **Read Luke 9 v 28-31.** "Departure" (v 31) is literally "exodus". How did Jesus (and Moses) view what he would do when he reached Jerusalem?

- **Read Mark 15 v 25-39; John 19 v 28-37.** At the beginning of John's Gospel, John the Baptist identifies Jesus as "the Lamb of God" (John 1 v 29). How do these two accounts of Jesus' death show how Jesus is "the Lamb", achieving a new "exodus"?

9. What was Israel enabled to do (Exodus 12 v 31-32)?

- The word "worship" (v 31) is the same as the one translated "slavery" in 2 v 23 (and elsewhere). How does this help us to know what we mean when we think of God's rescue as bringing us from slavery to freedom?

▶ **Read Exodus 12 v 40 – 13 v 16**

10. What are the people to do, when, and why?

Vigil (12 v 42): watch.
Consecrate (13 v 2): mark out as belonging to God.
Aviv (v 4): month in the Hebrew calendar; it falls around springtime.

⊡ apply

The night before he died, Jesus redefined the Passover meal as being a meal about him, and his death.

11. How does Exodus 13 help us to know why we share the Lord's Supper, and what we should be thinking about and speaking about as we do it?

12. Why do we find it hard to believe that serving God is true freedom? How can we use the events of these chapters to help us live in true freedom?

⊡ getting personal

Reflect on the idea that God's people are redeemed from slavery, for slavery. How should this shape your view of yourself as a member of God's redeemed people?

⬆ pray

Thank God:

- that his plans always prevail and his promises are always kept.
- that the lambs' blood on the doors was a preview of the blood of the greater Lamb, shed for you on the cross
- that God has designed you to experience the freedom of obeying him.

Ask God:

- to mercifully soften those you know who are hard-hearted
- to enable you to have an even greater sense of awe and joy when you next celebrate the Lord's Supper.
- to remember that obeying God is true freedom next time you are tempted to disobey.

4
Exodus 13 v 17 – 15 v 21
THROUGH THE SEA

The story so far

The Israelites are numerous, but enslaved and killed by Pharaoh in Egypt. One baby, Moses, is rescued from death, and, as an adult, flees to Midian.

God appears to Moses, reveals his name, and sends him to tell Pharaoh to let Israel go. Pharaoh refuses. It's now a contest between the LORD and the king.

Through the plagues, God shows his power. He judges each house through the firstborns' deaths, providing a lamb's death as a way out. Pharaoh lets Israel go...

⊕ talkabout

1. Why are songs great ways to remember things?

• How can singing something change the way we are feeling?

⊕ investigate

God's people will end this section singing—but first, they need rescuing.

> **▶ Read Exodus 13 v 17 – 14 v 12**

2. Why does God tell his people to turn back and camp on the edge of the Red Sea (v 1-4)?

DICTIONARY
Glory (14 v 4): honour.

3.   What does the Egyptian response show about how much they have learned in the plagues (v 5-9)?

• What does the Israelite response show about how much they have learned (v 10-12)?

▶ **Read Exodus 14 v 13-31**

4.   How does God both save his people and judge his people's enemies (v 15-30)?

5.   **Read Isaiah 43 v 16-19.** Isaiah is prophesying around 700 years after the exodus. What does God, through him, point the people back to? Then what does he tell them to do, and why (v 18-19)?

6.   In Mark 10 v 38, Jesus describes his death as "the baptism I am baptised with". He pictures his death as immersion in water. How does Jesus' death and resurrection mirror both the experience of the Egyptians and the Israelites at the Red Sea?

getting personal

Imagine the walls of waters collapsing in on one another, with people and horses being tossed about and dragged down into the depths. This is what Jesus stepped into at the cross. Jesus plunged into the chaos of the waters of judgment so that we can walk through on dry ground.

Imagine the people of God standing, safe on the shore, watching God's judgment unfold before their eyes. This is what you are doing as you watch, with the eyes of faith, God's Son hanging on the cross.

How does thinking about the cross make you feel:
• about Jesus?
• about yourself?
• about your future?

How will you make time this week to praise Jesus for what he did for you?

⊕ apply

7. How did the Israelites respond to what they saw at the Red Sea (Exodus 14 v 31)? What does this look like for God's people today?

⊕ investigate

In his first letter to the Corinthians, Paul says that the Israelites "were all baptised into Moses in the cloud and in the sea" (1 Corinthians 10 v 2). Led by Moses, they passed through the waters of death and came out to freedom.

Our baptisms are the same. "All of us who were baptised into Christ Jesus were baptised into his death" (Romans 6 v 3). Jesus has passed through the waters of judgment on our behalf. So we walk through life with our judgment behind us. We stand on the eastern side of the sea.

So what are we to do in response?

❯ Re-read Exodus 14 v 10-14

8. What do the Israelites need to do, and not do (v 13-14)? What will God do?

• What does it mean for us to do each of these today?
• Do not be afraid.

• Stand firm.

• Be still.

❯ Read Exodus 15 v 1-21

9. Why is singing a great response on the eastern side of the sea? How would you describe the emotional pitch of the song?

DICTIONARY

Exalted (v 1): held in high regard.
Stubble (v 7): plant stalks that stick out of the ground once grain has been harvested.
Mountain of your inheritance (v 17): the promised land.

10. What aspects of God's character and actions do the Israelites celebrate?

● How do verses 13-17 show trust in God for the future because of his actions in the past?

📖 **explore more**

▶ **Read Revelation 15 v 1-4**

Where are God's people standing (v 2)?
Who has been defeated (v 2)?
How do God's people respond (v 3-4)?

optional

Remember, the events at the Red Sea set up a pattern that was fulfilled in Jesus' death and resurrection. The event we are to look back to is Good Friday—Easter Sunday.

11. Re-write the Israelites' song to celebrate God's greatest act of deliverance.

⊖ apply

12. When do you find it hardest to be unafraid... to stand firm... or to be still?

• What do we need to sing to ourselves, and to each other, in those moments? In what ways can you do this?

⊡ getting personal

Whatever our circumstances, we can still sing of God's goodness, for we stand on the eastern side of the sea. How and what will you sing today, and when will you most need to sing it?

⊕ pray

Base your prayers on these three commands from Moses:

Do not be afraid.

Stand firm.

Be still.

Thank God for what he has done to enable you to live this way, and ask him to help you in the moments when you struggle to.

5

Exodus 15 v 22 – 18 v 27
TROUBLE ON THE ROAD

The story so far

God appears to Moses, reveals his name, and sends him to tell Pharaoh to let Israel go. Pharaoh refuses. It's now a contest between the LORD and the king.

Through the plagues, God shows his power. He judges each house through the firstborns' deaths, providing a lamb's death as a way out. Pharaoh lets Israel go...

... but when Pharaoh pursues Israel, God parts the Red Sea to allow his people to escape, and closes the waters on the Egyptians. Israel praises and trusts God.

⊕ talkabout

1. What do you most often grumble about? To what extent is your grumbling justified, do you think?

- Does grumbling make you feel better, or worse? Why?

⊕ investigate

The Israelites have been rescued from Egyptian slavery in the most dramatic fashion. They have seen the hand of God parting the Red Sea and defeating the Egyptian army. They have sung, "The Lord is my strength and my defence ... In your unfailing love you will lead the people you have redeemed" (15 v 2, 13). But all that was three days ago...

❯ Read Exodus 15 v 22-27

2. Why do the people grumble? How does God respond?

• Is Israel's grumbling justified, do you think?

❯ Read Exodus 16 v 1-36

3. How is the grumbling in this desert worse than the grumbling at Marah? How does God respond?

• Is Israel's grumbling justified, do you think?

4. God only gives enough for today, and not for tomorrow as well. In what way is this designed to cause the Israelites to trust him?

- God instructs the people to gather double the day before the Sabbath, and nothing on the Sabbath. In what way is this designed to cause the Israelites to trust him?

- What does Israel's response show about their view of God (v 19-20, 23-27)? What does this view look like in our time and culture?

▶ **Read Exodus 17 v 1-7**

5. How is this episode similar to the previous two?

- When the people grumble against Moses, how are they treating God (v 7)?

6. Draw the layout of the scene described in verses 5-6.

The choreography matters. The Israelites have put God on trial through their grumbling. And so the courtroom is arranged. The representatives of Israel are on one side (v 5). God says, "I will stand there before you by the rock at Horeb" (v 6). So God is on the other side. This is the case of Israel versus God. In the middle is Moses with his staff, and we're reminded that this is the staff that brought judgment on Egypt (v 5). So Moses is, as it were, the judge. All this takes place "in front of the people"—they are in the public gallery, so that everyone can see what happens.

7. Who should be struck by God's judgment? Who is struck, and with what result?

• **Read 1 Corinthians 10 v 4.** In what sense is Christ our "rock"?

⊡ explore more

optional

▶ **Read Psalm 95**

This psalm contains God's reflections on these episodes in the wilderness.

What was the grumbling a sign of (v 8)?
What were the people doing when they grumbled about God's plan and provision (v 9)?
What did it lead to (v 10-11)?
How does this psalm show the link between grumbling, sin, disbelief and judgment?
What should we do instead of grumbling (v 1-2, 6-7)?

➔ apply

8. Why is grumbling spiritually serious? As a congregation, do you tend to help each other stop doing it, or help each other keep doing it? How?

9. **Read Romans 8 v 28-32.** What is the Christian antidote to grumbling given in these verses?

⊡ getting personal

Reflect on your answers to Questions Eight and Nine.

How would trusting that God is working to make you more like Jesus transform your reaction to momentary inconveniences, and to any life-shaping issues you are wrestling with? How might it change the way you chat with other Christians who are going through hard times?

⊥ investigate

Now two nations enter the story: the nation of the Amalekites, followed by Jethro, Moses' father-in-law and the representative of the Midianites.

> **Read Exodus 17 v 8 – 18 v 27**

10. How do the Amalekites react to Israel's appearance (v 8)? What does Moses know is really going on behind their decision (v 15-16)?

> **DICTIONARY**
>
> **Altar (17 v 15):** stone table where sacrifices were made.
> **Decrees (18 v 16):** laws.

• What is the result for the Amalekites (v 13-16)?

So the end of chapter 17 shows us what the nations face because they oppose God's people and so lift hands against God: they face judgment. Then chapter 18 comes as a contrast—because next, we witness a representative of the nations joining God's people to worship God.

11. How does Jethro react to Israel's rescue (18 v 9-11)?

• What do the Israelites and this Midianite do together (v 12)?

Don't rush past this moment. This is the climax of the exodus. So far in the story we've had people treading on holy ground. We've had spectacular plagues of blood, frogs, gnats and hail. We've seen the death of every firstborn Egyptian. We've had pillars of cloud and fire connecting earth and sky. We've seen a road through the sea with walls of water on either side. We've had manna appearing from heaven.

But the climax of all this astonishing drama is a meal—a meal in the presence of God to which the nations are invited. And this is the climax because this is what endures. The dramas come and go. They live on only in the memory. But the meal continues. The presence of God continues.

12. **Read Matthew 26 v 26-29.** What did Jesus encourage his disciples to look forward to as they shared this Passover meal (v 29)?

⊟ apply

13. Do you (individually and as a church) tend to view "the nations":

- with suspicion, assuming they will hate you and need to be kept at arm's length?

- with optimism, ensuring that you avoid your local community criticising or hating you in any way?

- with surprise, because the community does not seem to welcome your church's presence?

How does Exodus 17 v 8 – 18 v 27 both reshape your expectations and challenge your behaviour?

⊡ getting personal

Do your answers to question 13 prompt you to pray differently, or to act differently, or to speak differently?

⬆ pray

Thank God that, because you have all you need in Christ, there is no need to grumble. Acknowledge that there is also no excuse for your grumbling. And ask him to show you where you have a grumbling attitude, and for help to see it as a spiritual issue and to work to know joy and contentment instead.

Thank God that he calls unlikely people in unlikely places to become part of his people. Pray that you would avoid being fearful, naive or arrogant in your view of those who are not following Christ.

6

Exodus 19 – 24
YOU SHALL...

The story so far

Through the plagues, God shows Pharaoh his power. He judges through the firstborns' deaths, providing a lamb's death as a way out. Pharaoh lets Israel go...

... but when Pharaoh pursues Israel, God parts the Red Sea to allow his people to escape, and closes the waters on the Egyptians. Israel praises and trusts God.

Israel fails to trust God, grumbling against him and Moses. God enables them to defeat the Amalekites, and Moses' father-in-law, Jethro, chooses to praise God.

⊕ talkabout

1. When and why is the rule of law a good thing? When and why is it a negative thing?

• How do you feel about obeying God's Old Testament law?

⊕ investigate

> **Read Exodus 19 v 1-25**

2. **Read Exodus 3 v 11-12.** What is the huge significance of the details of 19 v 1-2? What do they tell us about God?

DICTIONARY

Sinai (v 1): aka Horeb.
Priests (v 6): God's representatives to his people.
Abstain (v 15): refrain from.

3.   What has God done for his people? What does God call his people to do in response (v 4-5)?

• How does God describe Israel's identity (v 5-6)? Put each description into your own words.

4.   What do the instructions of verses 10-15 and 20-24, and the experiences of verses 16-19, show about whether and how God can dwell near people?

The New Testament uses some of the events and words of Exodus 19 to describe God's people after the life, death and resurrection of Jesus.

5. What has not changed for us, compared with God's people in the time of Exodus? **Read 1 Peter 2 v 9-11.**

• What has changed for us? **Read Hebrews 12 v 18-24.**

⊡ explore more

optional

▶ **Read Hebrews 12 v 25-29**

How does the writer link the future of this world to the experience of Israel at Sinai?

With Sinai in our minds' eye, and appreciating that we have been invited to a greater mountain—the heavenly Zion—how should we respond (v 25, 28-29)?

How should Exodus 19 and Hebrews affect the way we feel as we get out of bed on Sunday morning and get ready to go to church?

⊟ apply

6. How does your view of God, and your thinking about dwelling with God, compare with the way he reveals himself in Exodus 19?

- How does your view of and commitment to God's people—your church—compare with God's view in Exodus 19 v 5-6?

⊕ investigate

If we love God, we will desire to obey him—and so we will read chapters like the ones that follow asking: Should Christians obey these commands? Should we try to enforce them in society? How should we relate to the Law of Moses?

First, we need to recognise that these laws were given to people at a different time in a different culture, which was based on an agrarian economy.

Second, and even more significantly, the Law of Moses was given to people as part of the "old covenant". We live under what Jesus called the "new covenant" (Luke 22 v 20). We are living in a different stage in the history of redemption.

7. **Read Hebrews 8 v 7-13, Romans 7 v 6 and Galatians 6 v 2.** What difference does the new covenant make?

So does this mean we can ignore the pages of the Bible that set out God's Old Testament law? The answer is emphatically no. In discussing how the relevance of the law of the Sabbath had become a matter of dispute, Paul wrote, "Everything that was written in the past [in the Old Testament] was written to teach us" (Romans 15 v 4). We may not have to obey the letter of the law, but the law still matters—and it does so in three ways.

❯ **Read Exodus 20 v 1-21 and Mark 12 v 28-34**

DICTIONARY

Jealous (Ex 20 v 5): here, justly expecting what is his.
False testimony (v 16): lie in court.
Covet (v 17): crave; strongly desire to have.

8. How do the two greatest commandments (Mark 12 v 28-31) lie behind the Ten Commandments in the Law of Moses?

* **Read Exodus 21 v 28-29.** How do the two greatest commandments lie behind this command? So what timeless lessons are there for us in this command, even if we don't own a bull?!

Here is the first way God's law applies to us: **the law points us to God's timeless will.** We are to read the law of Moses and ask, "What timeless truths about God's will for his people's lives am I being pointed to here?"

9. **Read Romans 3 v 20-22.** What does the law do? What does it enable us to appreciate?

* Re-read Exodus 20 v 2-17 as a checklist by which you can assess your life. How does this exercise cause you to appreciate the great truth that in the new covenant, "now apart from the law the righteousness of God has been made known ... righteousness [that] is given through faith in Jesus Christ" (Romans 3 v 21-22)?

Here is the second way God's law applies to us: **the law points us to our need for a Saviour.** What the law does is expose our otherwise-hidden rejection of God.

10. Re-read Exodus 20 v 2-17 as a checklist by which you can assess Jesus' life. How does this exercise cause you to appreciate the holiness of Christ?

• **Read Matthew 5 v 17.** If the law points us to God's will, and to our need for a Saviour, how does Jesus "fulfil" the law?

Here is the third way God's law applies to us: **the law points us to the perfection of Christ**, in living the life we fail to, and in taking the punishment we deserve to.

> ⊡ **explore more**

> ▶ **Read Exodus 21 v 12 – 23 v 9**
>
> *What do all these laws have in common?*
> *How do the penalties differ if:*
> • *the wrongdoing is accidental?*
> • *the wrongdoing is deliberate but only attempted?*
> • *the wrongdoing is deliberate and committed?*
>
> Our crime against God—our sin—is both deliberate and committed.
>
> *What punishment is required—and how does Jesus provide it?*
>
> ▶ **Read Exodus 21 v 1-11 and 23 v 10-13**
>
> *What are these laws about?*
>
> We can sum them up as giving liberation and rest. And it is significant that they precede and follow the laws providing punishments for crimes. The restitution and punishment paid by Christ at the cross produces liberation and rest for his people.

▶ Read Exodus 24 v 1-18

11. What is the climax of this giving of God's law to God's people (v 1-2, 9-12)? How did Moses prepare for this (v 4b-8)?.

• **Read Luke 22 v 14-20.** How are we, once again, being pointed to the awesome and exciting nature of the Lord's Supper?

⊖ apply

12. How have these chapters:
• enlarged your view of God?
• increased your appreciation of Jesus Christ?
• reshaped your view of God's law in your life?

⊡ getting personal

How will your attitude towards God's law, your motivation for obeying it and your reaction to breaking it be different next week from what they were last week?

⬆ **pray**

Take each commandment in turn; briefly thank God for what it reveals of his will and his Son's perfection, acknowledge what it reveals about your own sinfulness and need for salvation, and ask for grace to live more according to God's will from now on.

7 Exodus 32 – 34
THE GOLDEN CALF: TRAGEDY AND MERCY

The story so far

Through the plagues, God shows his power and frees his people. When Egypt pursues Israel, God parts the Red Sea to allow his people to escape.

Israel fails to trust God, grumbling against him and Moses. God enables them to defeat the Amalekites, and Moses' father-in-law, Jethro, chooses to praise God.

At Mount Sinai, God meets with Israel in awesome power, explains their new identity as his people, and gives them his laws.

⊕ talkabout

1. When is compromise dangerous? When is it inexcusable?

• In those situations, why is compromise often still attractive?

⊕ investigate

▶ Read Exodus 32 v 1-6

2. What do the people do? Why?

• What does Aaron do? Why?

3. What do you make of the decision of the people, and of Aaron?

• **Read Psalm 106 v 19-22 and Romans 1 v 25.** What did God's people make of it, generations later?

• **Read James 4 v 4.** How is this a good description of what Israel does in Exodus 32?

getting personal

What difference would it make to your life if you viewed your sin as idolatry, and recognised idolatry as adultery?

❯ Read Exodus 32 v 7-35

4. Why does God not destroy his idolatrous, adulterous people (v 7-14, 30-34)?

5. How do the events of verses 15-30 show the seriousness of idolatry?

⊡ apply

The choice of the idol-shape is not arbitrary. The word translated "calf" need not mean a young cow, and Psalm 106 describes it as a bull. A bull was a common symbol of strength and fertility in surrounding nations. Israel is adopting the images of the surrounding cultures to re-imagine God.

The people are happy to worship God, but they want to worship him on their terms. They are happy to worship God, but they want to combine this with worldliness and indulgence. They let the nations set the agenda. They want a god who is visible and manageable. Even if they are not replacing God, they are reducing him.

6. What are the "golden calves" that we are attracted to? Why are they harder to spot in our own culture than in other cultures?

- How does Exodus 32 show us:
- the different ways in which we might compromise in our relationship with God?

- the dangers of doing this?

- the inexcusability of doing this?

⊡ investigate

❯ Read Exodus 33 v 1-17

7. What will God do for the people, and what won't he do (v 1-6)?

- How do verses 7-11 show why the people "began to mourn" (v 4) when they heard what God had said?

Are you in any danger of wanting God's blessings—forgiveness, being part of his church, eternal life—but not wanting God himself?

What truths about God that you've seen in Exodus are you going to use to help you to love God more than you love what he gives you?

In verses 12-17, Moses enters into conversation with God on behalf of the people. The word "you" in verse 14 is singular.

8. What is amazing about Moses' response in verses 15-16 to God's promise to him in verse 14?

• What does it tell us Moses cares about most?

▶ Read Exodus 33 v 18 – 34 v 7

Moses wants God to show him his glory—his "God-ness" (33 v 18). He wants to see God, to know what he looks like. But instead, God proclaims his name, his character. Instead of revealing how he looks, God provides a description of the way he is.

9. So what is the glory of God (34 v 5-7)?

This is our great hope—the merciful name of God. But there's still an unresolved tension. For God is also just. "He does not leave the guilty unpunished." This is our great problem—the holy judgment of God.

10. **Read John 1 v 17 and Romans 3 v 25-26.** How is the tension in the glory revealed to Moses resolved by the life and death of Jesus?

optional

⊡ explore more

Moses had broken the stone tablets with God's law written on them, as a visual sign that Israel had broken their covenant with God (32 v 19). Now God tells Moses to take two new tablets of stone up the mountain with him, because God is going to reaffirm his covenant (34 v 1, 4, 10). And in verses 10-28, God repeats a selection of laws, which are all designed to help Israel live as his people, faithful to him.

▸ Read Exodus 34 v 8-28

How would the laws mentioned in each of these sections help?
- *v 11-12*
- *v 13-15*
- *v 16*
- *v 18-26*

What do you think these laws reveal about the will of God for his people, on which we need to base our decisions as his people today?

▸ Read Exodus 34 v 29-35

DICTIONARY

Radiant (v 29): shining.

11. What effect does "seeing" God's glory, through hearing God's words on the mountain and in "the LORD's presence" in the tabernacle, have on Moses?

• **Read John 1 v 14, 18 and 2 Corinthians 3 v 7-8, 18.** Who can be transformed by the Lord's presence today? How?

⊡ apply

12. What might it look like for you to be transformed by seeing the glory of God in Christ this week?

• How can we use this glimpse of the glory of God in Exodus 34, and the greater sight of the glory of God in Jesus, to undermine the attraction of compromise?

⊡ pray

Confess to God the created things that you tend to turn into an idol and worship.

Thank God for the ways in which Moses' conduct in these chapters point you to Christ's work for you.

Use Exodus 34 v 6-7 to praise God for his glory.

8

Exodus 25 – 31; 35 – 40

AT HOME WITH GOD

The story so far

Having been rescued from slavery in Egypt by the LORD, Israel fails to trust him, grumbling against him and Moses.

At Mount Sinai, God meets with Israel in awesome power, explains their new identity as his people, and gives them his laws.

The people choose to worship a calf-statue instead of the rescuing God. Moses convinces God to have mercy on them, and sees—or rather, hears—God's glory.

⊕ talkabout

1. When someone walks into your living room, what impression of you and your life do your fixtures and fittings give?

⊕ investigate

It is time to rewind our focus a little, and rejoin Moses during the forty days he spent on the mountain-top; at the end of which, as we've seen, the people worshipped a golden calf instead of (or as well as) the LORD.

> **Read Exodus 25 v 1 – 26 v 30**

2. What do the Israelites need to offer to God, and what are these offerings for (25 v 1-9)?

DICTIONARY

Onyx (v 7): type of beautiful stone.
Ephod (v 7): garment worn by priests in the tabernacle; like a bib.
Tabernacle (v 9): a tent.
Cherubim (26 v 2): angels; God's warrior-messengers.

• What is exciting about verse 8?

A "tabernacle" is a tent. God dwelling in a tent may seem strange, but of course at this point in their nation's history, to the Israelites a tent meant only one thing: home. God had come down to visit on Mount Sinai; but now, he was moving into the neighbourhood.

So, what is God's home like?

3. Fill in the table to see how God's tabernacle is a picture of the Garden of Eden.

GENESIS	EXODUS	THE LINK
2 v 12	25 v 3-7	
2 v 9	25 v 31-39	
1 v 3, 6, 9, 14, 20, 24, 26	25 v 1; 30 v 11, 17, 22, 34; 31 v 1, 12	
2 v 1-3	31 v 12-17	
2 v 21-22; 3 v 8	25 v 8	

4. What does the furniture in the tabernacle tell us about God and his home?

• The ark, 25 v 10-22, especially v 16, 22. (Hint: The ark has the same proportions as the footstool of an ancient king.)

• The table (25 v 23-30)

• The lampstand (25 v 31-40—Hint: Read Psalm 119 v 105 and think about what a light does.)

▶ **Read Exodus 26 v 31-37**

5. What is to be woven onto this curtain? Where is it to be hung?

• **Read Genesis 3 v 24.** What is significant about the picture of the cherubim on the curtain, and its placement in the temple?

The tabernacle shows how wonderful it is to live at home with God—but it also bars the way to God. The layout of the tabernacle displays the wonder of the presence of God, but it also underlines the problem that we cannot stand in the presence of God.

6. **Read John 14 v 2-3.** Jesus is talking the night before he died. How does the tabernacle layout and furniture help us to appreciate the wonder of his promise here?

• **Read Matthew 27 v 50-51.** What did Jesus' death achieve?

⊡ apply

7. What difference would it make if you were more assured of, and more excited about, your eternal home?

⊡ explore more

optional

In Exodus 28 – 30, God moves on to describe the role of the priests, who will minister in the tabernacle.

❯ **Read Exodus 28 v 1 – 29 v 46**

What must they wear (28 v 4)?
What is the significance of the ephod and breastplate (v 12, 17-21, 29-30)? What does this tell us about the role of the priest?
How are the priests prepared for their duties (29 v 1-4, 10-28)?
What will the work of the priests enable to happen (v 42-46)?

❯ **Read Hebrews 9 v 11-14, 23-28**

How is the work of the Old Testament priests a picture of the greater work of our priest, the Lord Jesus?

⬇ investigate

In Exodus 32 – 34, as we have seen, the people worship the golden calf, Moses pleads successfully for mercy, and God reveals his glory to him. In 35 v 1 – 40 v 33, the tabernacle is built, just "as the Lord commanded" Moses (40 v 19, 21, 25, 27, 29, 32). "And so Moses finished the work" (v 33)—and so we reach the last few verses of the book…

> **Read Exodus 40 v 34-38**

8. How are these verses a fitting end to the book as a whole, and to the chapters detailing the design and building of the tabernacle?

• What is the only problem with the presence of the cloud of glory (v 35)?

And so Exodus leaves us wanting and needing more. A tabernacle, and later a temple, full of God's glory but without any people in it is not the scenario God is after. The good news is that Exodus is not the end of the story…

9. **Read Luke 9 v 28-36.** What are the links between the events of Exodus 40 at Mount Sinai and the events recorded by Luke on this mountain? (It may help you to know that "departure" in v 31 is literally "exodus", and "shelters" in v 33 is literally "tabernacles".)

• Where is God's glory to be found, according to God (v 34-36)?

getting personal

This is the glory Jesus longs to share with us. Jesus prayed, "Father, I want those you have given me to be with me where I am, and to see my glory, the glory you have given me because you loved me before the creation of the world" (John 17 v 24). Jesus longs for you to be with him and see his glory. If that doesn't change your perspective on life, nothing will.

I don't know what the future will bring your way. There may be triumphs. There may be problems. There will be highs and lows, and most of it will probably be fairly mundane. But Jesus longs for you to be with him, and to see his glory.

How does this need to shape your thinking and feeling about the best, and the hardest, aspects of your life today?

10. **Read Ephesians 2 v 21-22.** How does Paul link the Old Testament tabernacle/temple with the New Testament church?

• If God's address in the Old Testament was "The Tabernacle, Sinai wilderness" and then "The Temple, Jerusalem", what is it now? Why is this exciting and challenging?

⊡ apply

11. How has the book of Exodus as a whole caused you to be:
- more in awe of God?
- more understanding of who God is?
- more grateful that you are part of his people?
- more excited about your life, your future and your church?

12. Sum up the message of this part of Israel's history in eight words.

⬆ pray

Use your answers to Question Eleven to praise God together and pray for one another.

Leader's Guide: Exodus

INTRODUCTION

Leading a Bible study can be a bit like herding cats—everyone has a different idea of what the passage could be about, and a different line of enquiry that they want to pursue. But a good group leader is more than someone who just referees this kind of discussion. You will want to:

- correctly understand and handle the Bible passage. But also…

- encourage and train the people in your group to do this for themselves. Don't fall into the trap of spoon-feeding people by simply passing on the information in the Leader's Guide. Then…

- make sure that no Bible study is finished without everyone knowing how the passage is relevant for them. What changes do you all need to make in the light of the things you have been learning? And finally…

- encourage the group to turn all that has been learned and discussed into prayer.

Your Bible-study group is unique, and you are likely to know better than anyone the capabilities, backgrounds and circumstances of the people you are leading. That's why we've designed these guides with a number of optional features. If they're a quiet bunch, you might want to spend longer on *talkabout*. If your time is limited, you can choose to skip *explore more*, or get people to look at these questions at home. Can't get enough of Bible study? Well, some studies have optional extra homework projects. As leader, you can adapt and select the material to the needs of your particular group.

So what's in the Leader's Guide? The main thing that this Leader's Guide will help you to do is to understand the major teaching points in the passage you are studying, and how to apply them. As well as guidance for the questions, the Leader's Guide for each session contains the following important sections:

THE BIG IDEA

One or two key sentences will give you the main point of the session. This is what you should be aiming to have fixed in people's minds as they leave the Bible study. And it's the point you need to head back towards when the discussion goes off at a tangent.

SUMMARY

An overview of the passage, including plenty of useful historical background information.

OPTIONAL EXTRA

Usually this is an introductory activity that ties in with the main theme of the Bible study, and is designed to "break the ice" at the beginning of a session. Or it may be a "homework project" that people can tackle during the week.

So let's take a look at the various different features of a Good Book Guide:

⊕ talkabout

Each session kicks off with a discussion question, based on the group's opinions or experiences. It's designed to get people talking and thinking in a general way about the main subject of the Bible study.

⬇ investigate

The first thing you and your group need to know is what the Bible passage is about, which is the purpose of these questions. But watch out—people may come up with answers based on their experiences or teaching they have heard in the past, without referring to the passage at all. It's amazing how often we can get through a Bible study without actually looking at the Bible! If you're stuck for an answer, the Leader's Guide contains guidance for questions. These are the answers to direct your group to. This information isn't meant to be read out to people—ideally, you want them to discover these answers from the Bible for themselves. Sometimes there are optional follow-up questions (see ⊗ in guidance for questions) to help you help your group get to the answer.

⊡ explore more

These questions generally point people to other relevant parts of the Bible. They are useful for helping your group to see how the passage fits into the "big picture" of the whole Bible. These sections are OPTIONAL—only use them if you have time. Remember that it's better to finish in good time having really grasped one big thing from the passage, than to try and cram everything in.

➔ apply

We want to encourage you to spend more time working at application—too often, it is simply tacked on at the end. In the Good Book Guides, apply sections are mixed in with the investigate sections of the study. We hope that people will realise that application is not just an optional extra, but rather, the whole purpose of studying the

Bible. We do Bible study so that our lives can be changed by what we hear from God's word. If you skip the application, the Bible study hasn't achieved its purpose.

These questions draw out practical lessons that we can all learn from the Bible passage. You can review what has been learned so far, and think about practical differences that this should make in our churches and our lives. The group gets the opportunity to talk about what they personally have learned.

⊡ getting personal

These can be done at home, but it is well worth allowing a few moments of quiet reflection during the study for each person to think and pray about specific changes they need to make in their own lives. Why not have a time for reporting back at the beginning of the following session, so that everyone can be encouraged and challenged by one another to make application a priority?

⬆ pray

In Acts 4 v 25-30 the first Christians quoted Psalm 2 as they prayed in response to the persecution of the apostles by the Jewish religious leaders. Today however, it's not as common for Christians to base prayers on the truths of God's word as it once was. As a result, our prayers tend to be weak, superficial and self-centred rather than bold, visionary and God-centred.

The prayer section is based on what has been learned from the Bible passage. How different our prayer times would be if we were genuinely responding to what God has said to us through his word.

1 Exodus 1 – 2
PEOPLE WITH A PROMISE

THE BIG IDEA

God keeps his promises to his people, and his plans cannot be thwarted—so we should live in awe of him, and by faith in him, meaning we obey him.

SUMMARY

This study covers:

- the background to the events in Exodus (1 v 1-5; Genesis 12; 15; 17).
- the fruitfulness of the Israelites (1 v 6-7).
- the increasing oppression of the Israelites by Pharaoh; and God's thwarting of his plans (1 v 8-22).
- Moses' rescue through the Nile and his upbringing by his mother, and then in Pharaoh's palace (2 v 1-10).
- Moses' flight to Midian after murdering an Egyptian slave-driver, and his time in Midian as a shepherd (2 v 11-25).

OPTIONAL EXTRA

Ask your group members to write down on a sheet of paper everything they can remember about the events of Exodus (they can do this in pairs or threes if you are leading a group who may not know much/anything of the book). Then ask them to put those events in chronological order, and then collect answers and write them up on a piece of flipchart paper. There may well be some gaps (particularly between the Red Sea crossing and the golden calf)! You might keep the flipchart sheet and refer back to it as you go through the sessions.

GUIDANCE TO QUESTIONS

1. Have you ever relied on someone's promise to you? What was it about

them that made you trust them? Did you ever worry that they might not keep it? Your group may discuss flippant examples, such as relying on a promise to keep an appointment and then hanging around for hours when the promise-maker forgot; or more serious ones, such as marriage promises or a doctor's promise, and so on. There are no wrong answers here—the idea is to see that we do rely on promises in day-to-day life, and deciding to do so means weighing up the trustworthiness of the "promiser".

2. Read Genesis 12 v 1-7; 15 v 1-21; 17 v 15-22. What did God promise, and to whom? To save time, you could split your group into three and give them a passage each, and then ask them to report back to the rest of the group.

- **12 v 1-7:** God promised Abram he would be made into a great nation, would be blessed, and would be the source of God's blessing to others (v 2-3); and that he would be given the land he was in (v 7).

- **15 v 1-21:** God promised Abram that his descendants would be numerous (v 5), that the land he was in would be given to him (v 7), and that his descendants would be ill-treated slaves in a foreign land before being rescued by God and enabled to return to this "promised" land (v 13-16). The extent of the land is also described (v 18-20).

- **17 v 15-22:** God promised Abraham a son by his wife, Sarai/Sarah (v 15-16), and that her descendants would be kings (v 16); and that the covenant (binding agreement) God had made with Abraham (in chapter

15) would also hold for his son and further descendants (v 19, 21), but not for Ishmael (Abraham's son by his wife's slave-girl, Hagar—see chapter 16).

So in Genesis 12, 15 and 17 God had made a promise to Abraham and sealed that promise in a covenant. There were two key components to God's promise:

1. The promise of a people—Abraham would become a great nation.
2. The promise of a land—Abraham's family would inherit the land of Canaan.

And God would bless all nations, by fulfilling all his purposes, through Abraham's family.

3. How is God keeping his promise in Exodus 1 v 1-7? At the beginning of the book of Exodus, the promise of a nation is being fulfilled. Verses 1-5 list the sons of Israel who came to Egypt. The total number who made that original journey 400 years previously was just 70 (v 5). But now, those 70 people have become a great nation. They have "multiplied greatly", so they fill the land (v 6-7).

4. How is God's promise-keeping threatened in these verses [v 8-21]? Trace the rising threat through these verses:

• v 8-11: Oppressive measures are imposed to prevent the Israelites becoming "even more numerous"—the people are enslaved.
• v 12-14: Pharaoh works the Israelites ruthlessly, so they will have no time for plotting rebellion or becoming more numerous.
• v 15-16: Pharaoh tells the Hebrew (i.e. Israelite) midwives to kill every newborn baby boy—if his plan succeeds, Israel will be wiped out in a generation.
• **In what ways is Pharaoh's plan thwarted?**

• v 12: The oppression does not work: the Israelites remain fruitful and so their numbers increase.
• v 17-19: The midwives defy the authority of Pharaoh. They let the boys live and, when challenged, they claim the Hebrew women give birth before their midwives arrive.

5. How does Pharaoh raise the stakes (1 v 22)? He turns to genocide, ordering a general execution of all infant Israelite boys. Every Egyptian is conscripted to kill every Israelite newborn boy, by throwing them into the Nile to drown. **What is ironic about the way in which his plans are thwarted (2 v 1-10)?**

• This baby is placed in a basket on the River Nile (v 3), and is rescued from there (v 5). The river that Pharaoh wanted to bring death is the path to life.
• Pharaoh's own daughter rescues the baby, rather than killing him as her father had ordered (v 5, 10). Moses ends up living in the family of the man who wanted him dead (v 10).
• Moses is cared for by his own mother— and she is paid to raise her own son, straight out of Pharaoh's coffers (v 7-9)!

EXPLORE MORE
Israel's fruitfulness in Exodus 1 shows God is keeping his promise to Abraham. Read Genesis 1 v 26-29. How is it also a mark of Israel keeping God's command to all humanity? God had commanded humanity to be fruitful, increase in number and fill the earth (v 28—he repeated this when Noah left the ark, 9 v 1). Israel in Exodus 1 are "exceedingly fruitful"; they "multiplied greatly"; and the "land was filled with them" (Exodus 1 v 7). God's people are fulfilling the command of God.
Read Genesis 3 v 8-15. What had God

promised would be the relationship between the snake and the woman (v 15)? They would be in hostility to one another—and so would their "offspring" be. So there would always be rivalry between those who trust in God's promises (his people), and those who listen to the snake (everyone else). And one day, one of those who trusted God's promises would both be struck by, and would strike down, the snake.

How are Pharaoh's actions in Exodus 1 a fulfilment of the promise of Genesis 3 v 15? Pharaoh's hostility is one manifestation of the ancient hostility between the woman's offspring and the snake's "offspring". Pharaoh is trying to impede Israel's creative fruitfulness—and so he has set himself on a collision course with God. Both Pharaoh and God lay claim to Israel, though the nature of their respective rules is very different. One rule is oppressive and deadly; the other is liberating and life-giving.

What significance does this add to the coming showdown between Israel and Pharaoh? It will show us who wins, and whether or not God can be trusted to keep his promise of Genesis 3 v 15 and fulfil his purposes for humanity, such as multiplying and filling the earth. Exodus is not simply the record of the way in which two people groups treated each other, and which "won". It is the account of how God and the most powerful ruler in the world confronted one another—how in fact God and the snake confronted one another—and who won.

6. APPLY: What does Exodus 1 teach us about the promise-keeping of God? However bleak the setting, God is at work to keep his promises. He can be trusted to do what he has said he will do, even when we cannot see how he is working, and even when the keeping of his promise is a long

time coming from our point of view (as Isaac was for Abram, and as blessing was for Israel). **And the plans of powerful regimes?** God will not allow anyone to prevent his promises being kept. The most powerful ruler in our world can choose to defy God and seek to impede his purposes, but they cannot thwart God or prevent those purposes coming to pass.

- **How should this encourage us as God's people today?** When we face opposition—and when our brothers and sisters in other parts of the world face persecution—we can trust that God will keep his promises. The Lord Jesus promised, "I will build my church, and the gates of Hades will not overcome it" (Matthew 16 v 18)—and he will. Under Soviet communism, under Mao in China, and today in the Middle East, Satan has tried to destroy the church and prevent the preaching of the gospel. But each time God has demonstrated his sovereign power. Adapting Exodus 1 v 7, Christians have been "fruitful and multiplied greatly and become exceedingly numerous, so that the [earth is] filled with them." We can therefore obey God because we are confident in him and his ability to keep his word. (There is more on this theme in Q11-12.) We are being invited to seek to detect his hand in our own lives when we trust God's covenant promises. After all, Moses was kept safe in the place of violence and death. Here is sin at its most cruel and insane—and yet right here, the hand of God is at work. Even sin is a context in which God is at work, for he incorporates acts of sin into his purposes. That is what he is doing here; what he did when two other rulers opposed not his people but his own Son (Acts 4 v 27-28); and what he does in and around us still today as he works for our good in all things (Romans 8 v 28).

7. How are Moses' actions in 2 v 11-12 more "Egyptian" than godly? He treats another with violence, and responds to injustice with a greater injustice (he witnesses a beating, and murders the attacker). He behaves like an Egyptian slave master. He needs to unlearn the ways of the Egyptian court—it is a reminder that we cannot do God's work in worldly ways. **How do they undermine his ability to lead Israel (v 13-15)?** Because he loses the respect of the people (v 13-14), who don't recognise his leadership (v 14); and they force him to flee from Pharaoh, who now wants to kill Moses (v 15).

8. So in what sense has Moses left home, and in what sense has he come home? He has only ever known life in Egypt, in his mother's house in the Egyptian court. He has to leave all that he knows behind and flee to another country. But… he ends up in the area that God had promised to give Abraham's descendants, living with people who worship God. He is in the "home" God has promised to give his people. In leaving the only home he has ever known, Moses has come home. **Note:** Moses call his first son "Gershom". The tense of the verb in Moses' explanation of this name is ambiguous. The NIV translates it: "I have become a foreigner in a foreign land" (v 22). But the ESV fits the context better: "I have been a sojourner in a foreign land". The point is not that Moses is away from home, but that Moses has come home. Moses is enjoying rest and peace in the promised land. Despite Egypt being the place of his birth and upbringing, Moses now sees it as a foreign country.

9. By the end of chapter 2, to what extent has God kept his promises? What remains to be fulfilled?
• His people remain numerous, despite all Pharaoh's genocidal efforts. The promise of a great nation has come true.
• Moses has found a home in the promised land. The promise of the land is true for him, but the rest of the people are hundreds of miles away from it, in slavery.
• Moses has found blessing—safety and security, family and friendship in God's land. But again, the rest of God's people are far from blessing—being ruthlessly worked for a foreign king who wishes to wipe them out.

• **How do verses 23-25 suggest that God is about to intervene in Israelite history?** God "remembered his covenant with Abraham". What is going to drive this story is the promise to Abraham. "Remembering" is a covenantal term. It means deciding to act in order to fulfil a covenant. It's not that the promise to Abraham had somehow slipped God's mind. It's not that he got distracted by other things. "Remembering" means God is about to take the next step in the fulfilment of his promises. Verse 25 is literally, "God saw the people of Israel and he knew"—he knew their suffering and he knew his promises, and so now he would act to keep them.

10. Read Hebrews 11 v 24-27. Why did Moses choose to live as an Israelite, rather than an Egyptian? What did he give up in order to do so?
• Because he knew that the "pleasures of sin" are "fleeting". All the luxury of the Egyptian court would not last.
• Because he was "looking ahead to his reward"—he knew God's promises, and

trusted them, and so he knew that he had more and better ahead of him than he had left behind him.

- Because "he saw him who is invisible"—this is what Paul called living "by faith, not by sight" (2 Corinthians 5 v 7). Moses knew that, though he could not see God, God was there, and was trustworthy. So he obeyed the God who makes promises, even when it must have seemed impossible that those promises could be kept.

11. Re-read Exodus 1 v 15-18. Why did Shiphrah and Puah not obey Pharaoh? Because they "feared God". They held him in higher awe than the ruler of the superpower of their day, and they so trusted him to keep to his plans that they were prepared to defy those of Pharaoh. **What were they risking in order to disobey him?** Don't underestimate the pressure they were under or the risks involved in what they did. They stood to lose their lives.

12. APPLY: How do you face similar choices to Moses, and to Shiphrah and Puah? What would it look like for you to choose to fear God and live by faith, as they did? Whenever we are ordered or pressured to live in a way that disobeys God, either because of the power of the one who gives the order, or because of the allure of the lifestyle that disobedience offers, we are in the same position as Moses and the midwives were—needing to choose whether to fear God and trust God because we know he keeps his promises, or to forget God and trust ourselves or this world because we don't know the truth or the goodness of those promises.

Encourage your group not only to identify the times/circumstances in which they face these choices, but also to detail what fearing God and living by faith would actually involve. It may involve great risk or cost, of course—just as it did for Moses, and threatened to for the midwives.

2 Exodus 3 – 6
WHEN GOD GETS INVOLVED

THE BIG IDEA

God's personal name reveals that he is self-defining and eternally unchanging; so he can be trusted to keep his promises, and we can live courageously and do hard things for him, knowing he is with us.

SUMMARY

- God appears to Moses (3 v 1-10).
- God promises Moses that he will use him to rescue Israel and bring them to a good land; he reveals his name, "I AM

WHO I AM" (the LORD), which also reveals his character—self-defining, complete and unchanging, unconstrained by anything outside himself, and therefore able to make and keep promises (3 v 11-14).

- In a conversation between Moses and God, Moses makes objections, and God counters them with promises and then a challenge (3 v 15 – 4 v 17).
- Moses returns to Egypt; the people believe his message and worship God (4 v 18-31).
- Pharaoh responds to Moses' request to let

Israel go by announcing that he does not know the LORD, and oppresses Israel still more harshly (5 v 1-18).

- Israel and Moses complain to God (5 v 19-23).
- God repeats his promises to Moses (6 v 1-12).
- Moses and Aaron's belonging to Israel is established by their family tree (6 v 13-27).

OPTIONAL EXTRA

Find the meaning of your group's names (there are many websites that can help with this). Discuss how much/little those meanings match the character of each individual. Explain that our names are usually chosen because our parents liked the sound of them, or because they have been passed down the family. But in the Bible, names denote an aspect of someone's character, look, or birth (Moses means "drawn out", which refers to how he was plucked out of the River Nile, but was also prophetic—God would use him to draw his people out of Egypt). And in this study, your group will be thinking about the name of God—a name that reveals who he is and what he is like.

GUIDANCE FOR QUESTIONS

1. What's the hardest thing you've ever been asked to do? Surveys suggest that speaking in public will be very high up on many people's lists—which means they have something in common with Moses in these chapters (4 v 10). Tell your group you'll return to these ideas question in Q8.

☑

- **Did you do that hard thing? What enabled you to do it, even though you found it hard?**
- **[And/or] What's the hardest thing you've ever done simply because you are a Christian—something that**

you'd never have done if you weren't a follower of Jesus?

2. Sum up the events of v 1-14 in a couple of sentences or a couple of pictures. Some of your group will prefer drawing than using words. And your group will draw out different emphases from the passage. Sharing what you wrote/drew is a great way to look together at the images, twists and surprises of these verses. Do just make sure that no one is adding details and then majoring on them!

3. What does God promise in this meeting with Moses?

- **v 7-10, 17:** That he is a God who sees, hears and is concerned about his people (v 7); that he has begun to act to rescue his people, and will bring them into a good, plentiful land (v 8, 17)
- **v 12:** That he will be with Moses; that the people will worship God at the mountain at which this meeting is taking place—Horeb (v 1), also known as Sinai.
- **v 18:** Israel's elders will listen to Moses.
- **v 19-22:** The king of Egypt—Pharaoh—will not listen to Moses (v 19), but after God acts to show his power, "he will let you go" (v 20)—and the Egyptians will give the Israelites items of value and clothing (v 21-22).

4. What do we learn about who God is and what he is like?

- **v 2:** The fact that God chooses to appear to Moses as a fire that does not burn up the bush is striking. A fire often draws us towards it (v 3), but we also know we need to keep our distance from it. So perhaps God appears in this way to highlight this need for distance, even as we are drawn to him and recognise our need for him. That's a key theme in the whole book (e.g. 19 v 10-13, 20-24).

- **v 5:** God is holy, and where God is is holy. God is not like us.

- **v 7:** God is close enough and cares enough to see and hear and be concerned. He is above us (holy) but he is also among us. He is transcendent and he is immanent.

- **v 12:** He is with us. Again, we see that though he is holy and utterly different to us, he is also close to us and is with us.

- **v 14 (use the footnote to help with this):** This is the most important part of this question—do spend time thinking and talking about this verse. His personal name (what he is called, in the same way that I am called Tim) is "I AM WHO I AM" (or, as the NIV footnote gives it, "I WILL BE WHAT I WILL BE"). This is a statement deliberately designed to burst our definitions. We normally say, "I am something". A father. A teacher. Lonely. Tall. But this statement circles back on itself. God is not defined by anything outside of himself. And because (as the need for the footnote suggests) the Hebrew verb used can refer to a past action, a present action or future actions, God's statement here is intentionally ambiguous. It could be translated:

  - "I have always been who I have always been." The God of Abraham, of Isaac and of Jacob (3 v 6) will act in a way which is consistent with his track record.
  - "I am who I am." God is self-defining rather than shaped by others or by his relationship with others.
  - "I will be who I will be." God will determine the future and/or God will be what matters in the future.

God's identity is unconstrained. He will be who he decides to be. He will do what he decides to do. God is radically free—free to be and do whatever he chooses. Or, to be more precise, God is unconstrained by external factors. Nothing and no one can force him to be or do anything against his will. But God is constrained by his own character and promises. He will always act in a way that is consistent with his holiness and with his word. This is our great hope, proved trustworthy through his actions in history.

- Because God is not constrained by others, we can be sure he can deliver.
- Because God is constrained by himself, we can be sure he will deliver.

This means God has the power to keep the promises he has made.

Note: Our English Bibles translate this personal name of God as "the LORD" (for more on this, see pagesΔ103 35-40 of *Exodus For You*).

- **v 15 (also v 6):** God is eternal and unchanging.

5. How will the character of God be proved by the actions of God? The real definition of God's name is going to be the exodus itself: "And this will be the sign to you that it is I who have sent you: when you have brought the people out of Egypt, you will worship God on this mountain" (v 12). God is saying, *The sign that I am God is that I will save my people.* God then says, "I am who I am"—or "I will be what I will be" before describing in verses 16-22 what he's about to do. *This is what I will be to you,* he's saying.

Moses will discover who God is through God's saving acts. God is self-defining, and he is about to provide a definition of his name—and that definition is the exodus. In the exodus we will see the holiness of God in his judgment on Egypt. We will see the power of God in his triumph over Pharaoh and the gods of Egypt. We will see the grace of God in the redemption of Israel. We will see the rule of God in his words on Mount Sinai. So the character of God is proved and revealed by the actions of God.

- **Think about the life, death and resurrection of Jesus. How is the character of God proved and revealed by the actions of God?**

6. What is Moses' worry in verse 11?

Moses feels inadequate because of his weakness ("Who am I?"), Pharaoh's power ("that I should go to Pharaoh") and the scale of the task ("and bring the Israelites out of Egypt?"). It is a very understandable question to ask! **How is God's response in verse 12 both not an answer to Moses, and also the best answer to Moses?** It is not an answer in the sense that it does not answer the question! Moses asks, "Who am I?" (as in "Who am I to be able to do this?") And God might have said, but doesn't say, *Moses, you're the ideal person. You were brought up in the Egyptian court. You have seen your people's suffering. And you have been protecting and providing for your flock for years. You can do it.* God's response does not tell Moses anything about himself, his abilities or character that fits him for the task ahead of him.

But it *is* an answer in the sense that God says, "I will be with you". God is the One who will make the difference. Moses does not need to have higher self-esteem; he needs a greater sense of God's presence. God does not boost his self-confidence; he gives him the confidence of knowing he has God alongside him—"I will be with you".

7. APPLY: Read John 8 v 54-59. What is

Jesus claiming about himself here? This is the middle of an argument between Jesus and the Jews (v 31, 48). The key verses to focus on are v 56 and 58:

- Jesus claims that Abraham looked forward to Jesus' day and rejoiced about it (v 56) —in other words, Jesus' day is the day when all God's promises to Abraham (e.g. Genesis 12 v 1-3) are fulfilled.
- When the Jews point out that Jesus is not yet 50, so how could he know what Abraham thought, and how could Abraham have known about him, Jesus gives an answer that is strange in its grammar: "Before Abraham was, I am!" (v 58). He is claiming to have been in existence before Abraham was. And even more than that, he uses the divine name from Exodus 3 v 14—I AM. Jesus is claiming to the be the eternal I AM. Abraham knew him because Abraham knew the LORD, and Jesus is the LORD.

- **Look over your answers to Q4. This is who Jesus is. How similar or different is that to how you tend to describe him, individually and as a church?**

There is no "right" or "wrong" answer to this question. But we often struggle either to remember his holy, mighty transcendence (so we think of him as our mate, but not as the LORD); or to appreciate his immanence (so we think of him as distant, uncaring and unreachable). And we might even end up defining him for ourselves, forgetting that he is utterly self-defining. Of some aspect of God's character or Christian truth we might say, "I don't like the sound of that" … "I just don't think Jesus is like that or would say that." It might be his judgment, or his sovereignty, or his sexual standards. We make God in our image and he becomes a fluffy Jesus—a god who suits our desires but cannot help us when we are in need. We think of God in the way we want to think of him.

8. APPLY: What do you find hard in the Christian life? How does Moses and God's exchange in v 10-12 both comfort and challenge you? This links back to Q1. We are called to do hard things, and we find it easy to excuse ourselves from them, or do them half-heartedly. Moses and God's interaction in these verses comforts us—God says, "I will be with you" (v 12). He is saying to us, *You can walk through life with me. You can base your sense of self in your knowledge of me—find your confidence and worth in knowing that I am there for you, and here with you. You can know that I am with you, and achievements and your failures will not affect that status.*

But this is also very challenging. Verse 10 has a sting in the tail, following God's great assurances and promises: "So now, go. I am sending you…" Often, we want God to solve our problems without us doing anything hard ourselves. We need to ask if he is saying to us not only "I have seen … I have heard … I am concerned" (v 7, 9) but also "I am sending you".

And it is challenging to realise that we cannot excuse ourselves from doing hard things because of a lack of time, abilities, etc. on our part. What matters is whether God is with us or not—and, by his Spirit, he is. This is what Paul meant when he said, "I can do all this through him who gives me strength" (Philippians 4 v 13).

EXPLORE MORE
What problems does Moses have with what God has asked him to do (v 1, 10, 13)?
• What if Israel's leaders don't believe him (v 1)?

• He is not good at speaking in public (v 10).
• He simply does not want to do it—he would rather the LORD "send someone else" (v 13).

What do God's responses show about himself, and about how he deals with his people?
• In response to Moses' first question, God offers him three signs (a staff that turns into a snake, v 2-5; a hand that turns leprous, v 6-7; water that turns to blood, v 8-9). These signs anticipate some of the events of the plagues and exodus—so it is the exodus itself that will be the sign of God's identity and power, and since the exodus anticipates the death and resurrection of Christ, this is the "sign" that should cause people to believe today. This is the "sign" we show people who do not know God, or who are doubting God.
• In response to Moses' second problem, God points out that he is sovereign over both people's ability to listen, and to speak (v 11); and he promises to help him (v 12). Again, Moses needs to learn to think less about himself and what he can and cannot do, and more about the God who will be with him, and all that he can do.
• In response to Moses request to send someone else (v 13), "the LORD's anger burned against Moses" (v 14). God does expect obedience from his people. When he calls us to go, we need to go. But even now, God graciously allows him to take his brother, Aaron, as his spokesperson (v 14-17).

9. What difference does God becoming involved make to his people's lives [in 5 v 1-23]? None, in verses 1-5, because Pharaoh does not recognise the authority of "the LORD" (v 2) and therefore refuses to let the Israelites go.

Then things get worse for God's people. In v 6-9, Pharaoh orders his overseers to "make the work harder" (v 9). They have to maintain their output of bricks, without being given the raw materials (v 10-14), and are beaten when they fail (v 14).

By verse 21, it is clear that Moses and Aaron's request has only succeeded in making Pharaoh angry with the Israelites, so that they now face death.

10. What does God add to his promises in 6 v 2-8?

- v 6: God will rescue his people through "mighty acts of judgment".
- v 7: They will be rescued so that they can become his own people.

- **How do verses 6-8 show us what it means to be "redeemed"?** It means…
  - someone else acting for you, to free you from slavery. So God will act for his people to free them from the Egyptian yoke.
  - being freed for something—to enter a new relationship with your redeemer. God will "take [them] as my own people" (v 7).
  - to live with your redeemer. God will bring them to the promised land, and give it to them (v 8).

How does this apply to God's people today? Encourage your group to see how this description of redemption applies to followers of Christ:

- God acted for us in Christ to redeem us—free us—from slavery and captivity to sin and death.
- God freed us to be in relationship with him, as his people, serving him joyfully instead of serving sin miserably.
- God is bringing us to his promised land, and will one day give us the new creation as a "possession".

Note: All this will show who God is—so he says, "I am the LORD" in v 2 and v 8, as if to say, *Here is what I will do to show you what I mean when I say I AM WHO I AM.*

11. How do the people respond, and why (v 9)? Do you think it's justified?

They are slumped so deep in discouragement that they are unmoved by this revelation of God's character and purposes. In one sense, it is entirely understandable. Things have got harder, not better, for them since God became involved. It must have looked very unlikely that he would keep his promises, and there must have been a real concern that for as long as God sought to free his people, the actual living conditions for his people would become still worse as Pharaoh continued to be provoked. But in another sense, their reaction is unjustifiable. If they knew God, they would know that he is utterly trustworthy, because he is the LORD, who can make a promise and know with utter certainty that he will keep it, because he is not constrained by anything outside of himself. In forming their perspective, they need to consider their "harsh labour" less and the LORD and his promises far more.

12. APPLY: Why are the times when following God makes life harder, not better, dangerous for our faith?

Because, as the Israelites did, we see our circumstances more clearly than we do our God. And we don't know God very well. So when things get harder, we wonder if God is really there, or really cares, or will really come through—and that's the kind of ground in which distrust and unbelief flourish.

- **What does this passage tell us we need to do when we feel as though**

God has abandoned us or is not worth following? If you're struggling to obey God, you don't need more will-power. You need to know God better. In the exodus, and in the cross and resurrection, we see the actions of God, which reveal the character of God:

- We have seen that he is the Lord who keeps his promises (see 2 Corinthians 1 v 20).
- We have seen that he rules his world. It didn't look like that at times in the exodus, nor at the cross—but in fact God's enemies "did what [God's] power and will had decided beforehand should happen" (Acts 4 v 28).
- We have seen that he is the LORD, who redeems his people, because he loves his

people and is the father of his people (Exodus 4 v 22).

Knowing God is what enables us to trust and obey God, even when life is hard.

- **Why do we have even less excuse than the Israelites for not listening to God's promises?** Because we live the other side of the exodus and, supremely, the cross and resurrection. These Israelites had seen some of God's presence and power, through the signs Moses gave them; within months, they would see far more in the plagues and the Red Sea being parted. We have seen still more—we have seen the cross and the empty tomb. That is the "sign" Christ gives us (Matthew 12 v 38-40)—we have no reason and no excuse for not trusting or obeying him.

3 Exodus 7 – 13
GOD V PHARAOH

THE BIG IDEA
The most important truth of our lives is that we have been rescued from slavery to sin and death by God, through the death of Jesus; and rescued for joyful obedience to him. We need to remember this great truth, and the Lord's Supper helps us do that.

SUMMARY
- God repeats his promises to use Moses and Aaron (7 v 1-7).
- Aaron's staff becomes a snake in Pharaoh's presence—a foretaste of the plagues; Pharaoh refuses to listen (7 v 8-13).
- The first nine plagues (7 v 14 – 10 v 29).
- The last plague is promised: the plague on the firstborn (11 v 1-10).

- God tells Moses how Israelite families can escape his judgment through the death of a lamb in place of the firstborn; the Israelites trust and obey (12 v 1-28).
- The last plague comes; Pharaoh lets the people go (12 v 29-42).
- God commands his people to remember what he did for them through celebrating the Passover Festival and Festival of Unleavened Bread each year (12 v 43 – 13 v 1-16).

OPTIONAL EXTRA
Ask a few group members to share which records they would choose as their "Desert Island Discs" and why. Play their selections to the group if possible. Music has a way

of taking us back to a particular event or era in our lives. This links to the idea of the Passover meal and the Lord's Supper as *aide-memoires*. Alternatively, you could ask each member of the group to bring along an object that evokes strong memories for them, and talk about it to the group.

GUIDANCE TO QUESTIONS

1. Of those that you can actively remember, what have been the two or three most important positive events in your life? Encourage short answers, rather than long, detailed personal histories! The key part of this question is the sub-question that comes next…

• **How often do you think about them? In what situations do you call them to mind, and how do they make you feel?** People often recall positive important events when things seem to be going wrong in life (e.g. during a bad day at work, someone might remember that she is married; a grieving son may look back on a particular experience he shared with his father long ago). Others of us tend not to remember the positive events in our past at all—we are very prone to live in the moment and forget everything else. But when we do remember, depending on the memory and our current situation, we will experience a range of emotions.

Explain to your group that the purpose of this question is to begin to introduce the theme of the study—that events in our past shape us and should shape our experience of our present, and that they need to be recalled to mind in order to do that. You could return to this question after Q10 or 11, pointing out that for Israel, as for Christians today, the most important event in our lives happened before we were born, and we are prone

to forget it—for Israel, the Passover; for God's people today, the cross.

⌄

• **What are the events that most shape your nation's sense of itself? How does it remember them? Why does a nation need such foundation events?** E.g. US Independence Day on 4th July, remembering US independence from British rule; in the UK, Remembrance Day on 11th November, remembering victory in the First World War and those who fought and died; in Australia and New Zealand, ANZAC Day on 25th April, with a similar purpose. These events give nations a sense of who they are, what makes them different from other nations, etc.

2. How has Pharaoh challenged God (5 v 1-2)? God has told Pharaoh to let his people go—Pharaoh has responded that he does not know this God, does not recognise his authority, and is not about to let the LORD tell him what to do. This is a declaration of defiance. **What has God promised about Pharaoh and his people (7 v 5)?** Egypt will know that "I am the LORD"—God's identity and authority will be revealed through the LORD's mighty deeds. The plagues are the answer to Pharaoh's question, "Who is the LORD?", and the means by which God keeps his promise to his people.

3. Fill out the table below as you look at the first nine plagues. See table on the next page.

4. Who hardened Pharaoh's heart? Three times we're simply told that his heart became hard (7 v 22; 8 v 19; 9 v 7). Three times we're told that Pharaoh "hardened his heart" (8 v 15, 32; 9 v 34). He does it to

Plague	Passage	Is a warning given?	How does the Egyptian court respond?	Is Israel protected?	What are we told about Pharaoh's heart?
Blood	7 v 14-24	Yes	Replicates sign		Became hard
Frogs	7 v 25 – 8 v 15	Yes	Replicates sign		Hardened by Pharaoh
Gnats	8 v 16-19	None	Fails to replicate sign		Was hard
Flies	8 v 20-32	Yes		Yes	Hardened by Pharaoh
Livestock	9 v 1-7	Yes		Yes	Was unyielding
Boils	9 v 8-12	None	Can't stand before Moses		Hardened by the LORD
Hail	9 v 13-35	Yes	Hardens their hearts	Yes	Hardened by Pharaoh
Locusts	10 v 1-20	Yes	Asks Pharaoh to submit		Hardened by the LORD
Darkness	10 v 21-29 (also 11 v 3)	Yes	Regards Moses highly	Yes	Hardened by the LORD

himself. Pharaoh chooses to go deeper and deeper into resisting God.

But there is more going on: God is hardening Pharaoh's heart (7 v 3-4; 9 v 12; 10 v 20, 27; 11 v 10).

So Pharaoh's heart is hardened because he hardens his heart; and because the LORD hardens his heart.

- **What does this tell us about God's control of everything, and about people's responsibility for their response to him?** We have to take both these perspectives seriously. Pharaoh determines his own actions, and is responsible for his defiance; yet God determines his actions, too, because he is in control of everything. God is sovereign,

and at the same time we are responsible. To put it another way, Pharaoh freely chooses to do what God has freely chosen that he would do. We choose, and are responsible for our choice, but our choice is not outside God's control.

Don't allow your group to get too hung up on this! The point is to see that the Bible teaches that both perspectives are true—Pharaoh is responsible for his choices (and so are we) and God is in control of everything. The Bible does not explain fully how these are both true—but you might like to point out that Jesus himself teaches both truths (e.g. Matthew 11 v 27 teaches God's sovereignty and v 28 is an invitation/command to people to respond).

5. How are the plagues an answer to Pharaoh's way of thinking? God is declaring that he is the only true God and the only relevant God. He is the only God who is worth obeying. Through the plagues, God is saying, "There is no one like the LORD [your] God" (8 v 10). God is going head to head with Pharaoh and Egypt's gods. It is God versus gods. And in the plagues, "the Lord … brought judgment on their gods" (Numbers 33 v 4).

The ten plagues systematically undermine Egypt's pluralist claims. They are a lecture against religious pluralism—the belief that all religions are valid—and personal autonomy—the belief that I have the right to live as I like. It is a curriculum with ten unforgettable lessons. And the message is clear: there is only one God.

6. APPLY: How do the plagues motivate and equip us to talk to friends who are happy for us to believe in "the Christian God", but don't believe they need to? Someone who is happy for others to believe in the Lord, but will not submit to him themselves, is living in defiance against him, and faces his judgment. The plagues remind us of the reality and severity of God's judgment against those who adopt Pharaoh's attitude ("Why should I obey him?"), and so they motivate us to make the effort and take the risk to challenge them. They also equip us to do so—we need to help our friends see that the claims of the "Christian God" are to uniqueness—not one option among many but the only option available—because the Bible presents us with a God who is the only true God, and who made everything and rules everything. He does not fit today's Western worldview—he explodes it. And we can point unbelievers to God's actions in history—the plagues in Egypt, and supremely, the resurrection of his

Son—which prove who he is (see Explore More below).

EXPLORE MORE
… Read Acts 4 v 8-22; Exodus 9 v 14, 16. What are the similarities between the purposes of the plagues and the purpose of the death and resurrection of Jesus Christ (Acts 4 v 10-12)? The question the Jewish Council ask is, "By what power or what name did you do this? "(v 7). It's an echo of Pharaoh's question, "Who is the LORD, that I should obey him?"
In v 10-12, Peter replies that the death and resurrection of Jesus is the sign that "salvation is found in no one else". His death and resurrection are the ultimate signs that God's judgment is real and his salvation is needed. Just as the plagues established the authority and uniqueness of God's "name" (Exodus 9 v 14, 16), so the resurrection establishes the authority and uniqueness of Jesus' "name" (Acts 4 v 12).
What is one indicator that someone understands the authority Jesus has (v 13, 18-20)? However "ordinary" you are (v 13), you courageously proclaim Christ's name to those around you, whoever they are and whatever the risk, refusing to be silenced by worldly power or intimidation (v 18-20). Once you grasp the meaning of Christ's cross and see God's salvation in Christ's resurrection, you "cannot help speaking of what [you] have seen and heard" (v 20).

7. [In Exodus 11 v 1 – 12 v 39] Which families face death, and why? Every family, because "every firstborn son in Egypt will die" (11 v 5). The reason why "the LORD makes a distinction between Egypt and Israel" (v 7) is because Israel are those who listen to him, and therefore obey his rescue plan. But the point is that the Israelites deserve the judgment of death just as much as the Egyptians. If Israel were undeserving of death, then they wouldn't need to kill the lambs and daub the blood on their door-frames. And ultimately, all are deserving of death because, as we've seen in the previous chapters in Exodus, all (Egyptians and Israelites) have failed to trust and love God—instead ignoring, defying, defaming or complaining to him. **Which families escape death, and how?** Trace the exact details of how a family escaped death:

- 12 v 3-5: Take a lamb, the amount to be sufficient for a portion for each person. The lambs must be without defect—the best of the flocks, not the worst.
- v 6: Having looked after the lamb, slaughter them on a particular day.
- v 7: Take some of the lamb's blood and put it round the door-frame of the house.
- v 8-11: Eat all the lamb, dressed ready to leave Egypt.
- v 12-13: This way, when God strikes down the firstborn in every household, "when I see the blood, I will pass over you" (v 13).

- **In what sense was there "not a house without someone dead" (v 30)?**
  In every home throughout Egypt and Goshen, the death count is the same. The following morning there is a corpse. The only question is: is it a lamb or is it a child? Who has died?

8. Read Luke 9 v 28-31. "Departure" (v 31) is literally "exodus". How did Jesus (and Moses) view what he would do when he reached Jerusalem? As an exodus. Jesus viewed his death as achieving a second exodus—a liberation from slavery, a substitutionary sacrifice that brought rescue from God's judgment of death.

- **Read Mark 15 v 25-39; John 19 v 28-37. At the beginning of John's Gospel,**

John the Baptist identifies Jesus as "the Lamb of God" (John 1 v 29). How do these two accounts of Jesus' death show how Jesus is "the Lamb", achieving a new "exodus"?
- Jesus died in the darkness (Mark 15 v 33)—the ninth plague that expressed God's judgment on Egypt was now showing God's judgment falling on him.
- The soldiers used hyssop, the plant that was used to daub the blood on the Israelite door-frames, to lift a sponge to Jesus' lips—a hint of the first exodus (John 19 v 29).
- Jesus' bones were not broken—he was an unblemished lamb, "prepared" for death in the same way as the lambs in Egypt were (v 33, 36—see footnote link to Exodus 12 v 46).

So Jesus is the Lamb in the sense that he is the One the first exodus pointed to. He was sacrificed as our substitute. We all deserve to die because of our rebellion against God. But Jesus has died in our place. His blood is, as it were, daubed over our lives so that God will "pass over" us when he comes in judgment.

As a result, we are redeemed. Like Israel, we are redeemed from slavery and death—but not from slavery in Egypt, but slavery to sin, and the penalty of death that our sin deserves.

9. What were Israel enabled to do (Exodus 12 v 31-32)? Pharaoh summons Moses and Aaron and pretty much commands the Israelites to leave, just as Moses had requested back in 5 v 1.

- **The word "worship" (v 31) is the same as the one translated "slavery" in 2 v 23 (and elsewhere). How does this help us to know what we mean when we think of God's rescue as**

bringing us from slavery to freedom?
We are presented with competing claims to the service of Israel. To whom does Israel belong? Both God and Pharaoh lay claim to Israel, though the nature of their respective rules is very different. Under Pharaoh's rule the Israelites experienced work without rest, the state-sponsored murder of children, the interference in family life and the confiscation of property. In contrast, to serve God is to find true freedom.

So Israel is liberated for obedience; and liberated through obedience—through obeying God by trusting in his rescue plan. It is the same for us as those who have been rescued through the Lamb, the Lord Jesus. We are not simply freed from slavery to sin. We are certainly not set free for a life of self-indulgence (Galatians 5 v 13). Instead, we have become slaves to righteousness (Romans 6 v 15-23). But this service leads to life. This slavery is freedom for we are liberated to be the people we are meant to be.

10. What are the people to do, when, and why? This double liberation from sin and death is, God says, to be commemorated in two festivals, annually. Passover starts on the 10th day of the month of Aviv and ends on the 14th day. The Feast of Unleavened Bread starts on the 14th day and ends on the 21st. The key day is the 14th, the day of liberation. The two festivals essentially take place on the same day and commemorate the same event. But they each reflect a different aspect of its meaning. The Passover commemorates liberation from death since it re-enacts God's passing over Israel in his bringing of death to Egypt (12 v 43-49). The Festival of Unleavened Bread commemorates liberation from slavery since it re-enacts Israel's hasty

departure from Egypt (13 v 3-10).

There was a further act of remembrance—the consecration of the firstborn (13 v 1-2, 11-16). God had redeemed Israel. As such, they now belong to him. As we have seen, they are redeemed from slavery to slavery, albeit it a form of slavery which is experienced as freedom. God has bought Israel. So, as his redeemed firstborn son, Israel belongs to God. And this ownership is marked by the consecration or redemption of every firstborn male. Each of these acts of commemoration includes a moment when future generations are expected to ask about its meaning (13 v 8, 14). They do more than merely remember a past act. They are re-enactments of the story. People are not simply observers, but participants. So they incorporate future generations into the people of God. As the Passover Festival was kept, the Passover event became an act which future generations were part of. It became an act which continued to shape their identity as God's people.

11. APPLY: [The night before he died, Jesus redefined the Passover meal as being a meal about him and his death.] How does Exodus 13 help us to know why we share the Lord's Supper, and what we should be thinking about and speaking about as we do it? (If you have time, read Luke 22 v 1-23—notice how Luke mentions the Passover six times, in v 1, 7, 8, 11, 13, 15). Just as the redemption of Jesus, the Passover Lamb, is the fulfilment of the exodus, so the Lord's Supper is the fulfilment of the Feasts of Passover and Unleavened Bread.

And just as the Passover shaped the identity of the Israelites, so the Lord's Supper shapes our identity as Christians. We not only remember the story of the cross and resurrection. We enact it and participate in it. It becomes our story and our identity—our living reality.

Communion is our *aide-memoire*. It helps us to remember that, in Christ, we died to the reign of sin. Sin is no longer our master. We no longer obey its commands. Now we live as slaves to righteousness—a slavery that is true freedom.

12. APPLY: Why do we find it hard to believe that serving God is true freedom? Because we live in a world that defines freedom as not being influenced or directed by anyone or anything other than ourselves; and because we have hearts that naturally wish to rebel against God's rule, seeing it as oppressive and harsh rather than kind and life-bringing. We listen to the lies of the devil, just as Adam and Eve did in Eden (Genesis 3 v 1-6). **How can we use the events of these chapters to help us live in true freedom?** We are free from fear of the world—even a ruler such as Pharaoh is powerless compared to God, and never acts outside God's control, and therefore can never thwart God's plans. We are free from fear of death and judgment—Christ has died in our place, bearing God's judgment on our sin, so that we need never face that judgment, but can instead live as part of God's people eternally. We are free to enjoy obeying God—and it is obedience to God that proves to be the purpose for which we were made and what we were designed to find fulfilling.

We need to remember who we are, by remembering our exodus—the exodus Jesus accomplished in Jerusalem. So encourage your group to think specifically about how they will ensure they make the most of the *aide-memoire* of the Lord's Supper next time they participate in it.

Exodus 13 v 17 – 15 v 21

4 THROUGH THE SEA

THE BIG IDEA

God brought Israel through his sea of judgment and out the other side; and, in Jesus, we too have passed through the waters of judgment. We live with judgment behind us—we need not be afraid, can stand firm, and trust God as we sing in praise to him.

SUMMARY

- God leads his people to a place where they have the Red Sea at their backs (13 v 17 – 14 v 4).
- Pharaoh pursues Israel; Israel panics (14 v 5-12).
- Moses reassures the people (14 v 13-14).
- God parts the sea; Israel passes safely through, but the pursuing Egyptians are drowned as the waters close back over them. The people fear God and trust Moses (14 v 15-31).
- Israel, led by Moses and then Miriam (his sister), sing in praise and trust about all that God has done for them, and will do for them (15 v 1-21).

Note: More detail on what actually happened in history, and brief interaction with modern attempts to explain the events away, can be found on pages 100-103 of *Exodus For You*.

OPTIONAL EXTRA

End and/or begin this study by singing together as a group. Choose a song that celebrates how God delivers us through Christ's death and resurrection (see Q11). Print out the words ahead of the study, or choose a simple chorus that everyone knows the words to.

GUIDANCE TO QUESTIONS

1. Why are songs great ways to remember things? Singing something is more memorable than reading, listening to or even reciting it. Singing engages our hearts rather than only our memories. And when we sing, we are able to describe and display our emotions.

- **How can singing something change the way we are feeling?** Think about singing a national anthem before a major sporting event—it engenders pride, determination and unity. Or what about singing a familiar song to yourself under your breath when feeling scared or alone, and it causing you to smile? Or an army singing as they march into battle, to give them a sense of togetherness and courage. Or a couple singing their favourite song together, as a way of enjoying one another and their shared history.

2. Why does God tell his people to turn back and camp on the edge of the Red Sea (v 1-4)?

- So that they will be hemmed in against the sea (v 2) and Pharaoh will think they are confused and trapped (v 3).
- So that then Pharaoh "will pursue them", and God will gain glory by showing once

and for all that "I am the Lᴏʀᴅ" (v 4). This is to be the final act in the conflict between God and Pharaoh.

3. What does the Egyptian response show about how much they have learned in the plagues (v 5-9)? They have learned nothing. In v 5, Pharaoh changes his mind about releasing the Israelites (as he had after the seventh, eighth and ninth plagues, 9 v 27-29, 34-35; 10 v 16-20, 24-28). He still wants to retain the Israelites' "services"—he is determined that these people should serve him, and not the Lᴏʀᴅ. Nothing has changed—his hardened heart is still being hardened by the Lᴏʀᴅ (14 v 8).

- **What does the Israelite response show about how much they have learned (v 10-12)?** They have not learned very much either. When they see the Egyptian army, they are full of doubt and despair. They are terrified (v 10), because they gaze at the Egyptians and forget about God. They assume they will die (v 11). And they think that they would be better off not having been rescued by God. Their response here is not much different to their response to Pharaoh's opposition in chapters 5 – 6. They have witnessed the plagues and experienced the Passover, yet they still do not trust God when trouble comes or when life gets harder.

⌄

- **How can we as Christians today be very similar?** This will be picked up on in Q8: but how quick we are to think God is not with us, or for us, or powerful to help us, forgetting all that we know he has done in the past, supremely in Christ, and also in our own lives today. When life gets harder because we are Christians, what we have left tends to look very attractive.

4. How does God both save his people and judge his people's enemies (v 15-30)?

God separates the waters through sending "a strong east wind" (v 21), so that the Israelites can pass through the sea on dry ground (v 22). They reach safety on the other side of the sea—the side of the promised land, and the opposite side to Egypt (v 20-30).

But those same waters become waters of judgment for the Egyptians. God prevents the army from touching his people (v 19-20, v 24-25), and then lets the waters close over the Egyptian army (v 26-28). "Not one of them survived."

Notice that judgment takes the form of un-creation. Water and land were separated to allow the Israelites to pass through—now they un-separate, just as they did in the time of Noah (Genesis 7 v 11-24). Judgment takes the form of water, and salvation means being given a way through that water.

⊗

- **How had the men of Egypt been treating the males of Israel (Exodus 1 v 22)?** They had been drowning the baby boys of Israel in the River Nile.

- **How does this punishment in the Red Sea fit their crime?** They are now drowned in the Red Sea by the God of those baby boys. Those who are guilty of seeking to kill innocent children are now killed in the same way they would have killed those children.

5. Read Isaiah 43 v 16-19. Isaiah is prophesying around 700 years after the exodus. What does God, through him, point the people back to? Then what does he tell them to do, and why (v 18-19)?

Isaiah reminds the people of how God liberated the Israelites through the sea. But then God says, in effect, *Forget about that. I'm going to do it again—bigger and better.*

6. In Mark 10 v 38, Jesus describes his death as "the baptism I am baptised with". He pictures his death as immersion in water. How does Jesus' death and resurrection mirror both the experience of the Egyptians and the Israelites at the Red Sea?

Water is the symbol of judgment. The cross is the reality. At Calvary, the waters of judgment engulfed Jesus. He experienced what the Egyptian army did—death in the waters of judgment. And as he died, the land was covered in darkness. God pulled apart creation around Jesus, and Jesus sank into the tomb.

But on the third day Jesus rose again. God brings life out of death, salvation out of judgment, light out of darkness. Just as the Israelites passed through judgment, so did Jesus. He came out the other side of it. And he leads his people through, just as Moses did—in the person of his Son, God brings his people through the waters of death.

7. APPLY: How did the Israelites respond to what they saw at the Red Sea (Exodus 14 v 31)?

They looked at God's judgment on his enemies and they:

- "feared the LORD"—that is, had a right awe of his power and authority.

- "put their trust in him and in Moses his servant." They understood that the God of all creation was with them and for them, and that he had appointed and was working through Moses. They expressed their trust in God by trusting Moses.

What does this look like for God's people today? We, too, should fear God as we see the judgment and deliverance of the cross and resurrection of Jesus. And we, too, should trust him and his servant. We express our trust in God by trusting his Son as our Rescuer and Ruler.

8. What do the Israelites need to do, and not do (v 13-14)?

- Not be afraid (v 13)
- Stand firm (v 13)
- Be still (v 14)

What will God do?

- Bring deliverance (v 13)
- Fight for them (v 14)

- **What does it mean for us to do each of these today?** Make sure you think about why we are able to do each of the three commands, in light of the deliverance we have in Jesus. Your group might find it helpful to think about what the opposite would look like.

  - **Do not be afraid:** We do not worry that sin will defeat us, or that death will be the end of us, or that God might judge us after all. We are not scared of what life, or those who oppose our faith, might throw at us. How do we live without fear? We tell ourselves that we have already been pulled down to death and judgment has already overwhelmed us—in the person of Jesus. We died with him and we have risen with him. We need not fear death and judgment because we have already passed through the waters in Christ. "The Lord will fight for you," says Moses (v 14). Christ has taken on sin and death, and has given us the victory. No one can take it away from us.

  - **Stand firm:** It might be helpful to read Ephesians 6 v 12-13. We face the temptations of the world, the flesh and the devil (see v 12). And maybe we're tempted to capitulate and return to

slavery. Moses' word to us and Paul's word to us are the same: stand firm. "Put on the full armour of God, so that when the day of evil comes, you may be able to stand your ground, and after you have done everything, to stand" (v 13). Our armour is the gospel. It is faith in the finished work of Christ. Satan says, *You cannot resist me and you are mine.* And we say, *Yes, I can, and no, I'm not. I am Christ's. I am on the east side of the sea. I am no longer under the power of sin. I have gone through death and resurrection in Christ. And so I have a risen to a new life—and I am going to stand firm, whatever lies you may whisper to me.*

- **Be still:** We tend to react to difficulties either by relying on ourselves or by running away. We are to take responsibility for what is our responsibility—but we leave the rest to God. We don't run away from being a good parent, or confronting an issue at work, or witnessing to our neighbours, or confessing our sin. But we don't rely on ourselves to convert our neighbours, or to change or outmanoeuvre our boss, or to save our child. We must leave those things to God, and be still. Israel was called neither to run away from the most powerful army in the world, nor to seek to fight it—because God would fight for them. He will fight for us too, as we stand still and let him. When we try to take control of our world or of our eternal future, we're in effect saying, *God's not doing a good job so I'm going to step in.* The result is over-busyness, stress and unwise decisions, because we're not very good at doing God's job for him. We need to be still.

9. Why is singing a great response on

the eastern side of the sea? Because (see Q1) singing is a natural way to celebrate something, and display our feelings about something, especially when what we have seen or experienced is something that we struggle to find the words to describe. The events Israel have just witnessed fit that category! **How would you describe the emotional pitch of the song?** There's no right or wrong answer here, but your group may come up with: triumphant; grateful; joyful; trusting.

10. What aspects of God's character and actions do the Israelites celebrate?
- He is a mighty warrior who has fought for his people (v 1-6).
- He is the angry King who has defeated his enemies by engulfing them with the seas (v 8-10).
- He is the unique, incomparable God (v 11).
- He is the loving leader of his people, who will keep his promises to them (v 13-17).
- He is the eternally ruling LORD (v 18).

- **How do verses 13-17 show trust in God for the future because his actions in the past?** Verses 13-17 describe things the LORD has promised to do, but has not yet done—to lead his people through foreign lands, to cause the surrounding nations to be in awe of them, and to bring them to the promised land, the place of God's dwelling (v 17).
  So here, the Israelites are looking back at all that God has done, and therefore declaring that they trust him to do what he has promised to do in the future.

EXPLORE MORE
Read Revelation 15 v 1-4. Where are God's people standing (v 2)? As in Exodus 15, they are standing beside a sea.
Who has been defeated (v 2)? "The

beast and its image." The "beast" is the personification of anti-god state power, one of the weapons of Satan (in Revelation, the "dragon") in his cosmic battle against God. Don't miss the link to the Red Sea here, where the most powerful state in the world, whose ruler had sought to defy God, had been defeated.
How do God's people respond (v 3-4)? By singing—and tellingly, the song they sing is "the song of God's servant Moses and of the Lamb" (v 3); they sing Moses' song, but about the rescue through judgment that the Lamb, the Lord Jesus, achieved at the cross. We will spend eternity singing what Moses sang on the eastern shore. Point out to your group that we can and should sing this now, too. We have been judged in Christ, and saved in Christ. We have passed through the waters in him, and now we stand on the eastern shore, on our way home... and we sing.

11. Re-write the Israelites' song to celebrate God's greatest act of deliverance.
It could be something like this:
[1] I will sing to the Lord,
    for he is highly exalted.
Both sin and death
    he has hurled far away ...
[7] In the greatness of your majesty
    you threw down sin and death.
You unleashed your burning anger at the Calvary;
    it consumed Jesus like stubble.
[8] By the blast of your nostrils
    the waters of your judgment piled up.
The surging waters overwhelmed Jesus in my place
    the deep waters congealed in his heart
    for my sake ...
[17] You will bring your people and plant them in your new creation,

on the mountain of the New Jerusalem, your inheritance—
and you, O LORD, will make your dwelling among them.

12. APPLY: When do you find it hardest to be unafraid... to stand firm... or to be still? Encourage your group to be personal and specific.

• **What do we need to sing to ourselves, and to each other, in those moments? In what ways can you do this?** Again, encourage your group to be specific. It

may be that remembering a particular Christian song will help; or memorising some Scripture verses; or asking a friend to text a cross-centred encouragement at a particular point in the week. But crucially, we need consciously to sing the truths about who God is and what he has done for us in Christ—we need to be willing to "sing" this to others as and when they need it, and we need to be willing to listen to others who remind us of these truths.

5 Exodus 15 v 22 – 18 v 27
TROUBLE ON THE ROAD

THE BIG IDEA
(This study takes in two sections—
15 v 22 – 17 v 7, and 17 v 8 – 18 v 27.)
Grumbling is a way of suggesting that God is not trustworthy or generous—it brings judgment, which Christ takes for us, and it is God's provision in Christ that enables us to defeat it.
The nations respond to Israel then, and God's people today, either with enmity, which brings God's judgment, or with joy, which brings unity and blessing in the presence of God.

SUMMARY
• Israel grumbles about a lack of water—God provides water (15 v 22-26).
• Israel grumbles about a lack of food, wishing they were back in Egypt—God provides quail and manna, but the people fail to trust the way he tells them to collect it (15 v 27 – 16 v 36).
• Israel grumbles again, about a lack of

water—God provides water; he sets up a "trial" between Israel and himself, and he receives the strike from Moses' rod of judgment, even though it is Israel who deserve punishment for their lack of trust and questioning of God's goodness (17 v 1-7).
• The Amalekites oppose Israel, and are defeated (17 v 8-16).
• Jethro (a Midianite) celebrates God's rescue of Israel and eats with Israel's elders in God's presence (18 v 1-12).
• Jethro advises Moses on how to administer the law and judge cases (18 v 13-27), which prepares us for the giving of the law in chapters 19 – 24.

OPTIONAL EXTRA
Search the internet or letters to the editor pages of a newspaper to find a selection of complaints, gripes and grumbles about recent TV shows or news stories. Remove any direct references, and then read the

complaints aloud to the group—see if they can guess what is being complained about, and discuss whether the complaint is justified or not.

This links with one of the main themes of the study: grumbling.

GUIDANCE FOR QUESTIONS

1. What do you most often grumble about? To what extent is your grumbling justified, do you think? At this stage, there are no right or wrong answers—the aim is just to prompt people to think about their grumbling. It might be worth pointing out that we tend to think of grumbling as something that other people do. What we do is make justified complaints or offer constructive criticism, but we don't grumble! We make ourselves the exception—but the reality is that most of us grumble and some of us grumble most of the time.

You could return to this question either after the Explore More, or after Q7.

- **Does grumbling make you feel better, or worse? Why?** Again, there are no wrong answers, but don't let your group simply conclude that grumbling makes us feel better because we "get it off our chest". In fact, grumbling often makes us feel worse—it does not solve anything, often produces grumbling from others to add to our own, and reinforces a sense of discontentment or bitterness in us.

2. Why do the people grumble? Because they don't find water for three days (v 22), and then the water they find at Marah is undrinkable (v 23). Marah means "bitter"—and it's not just the water that is bitter; the people are too. **How does God respond?** He shows Moses a piece of wood which makes the water fit to drink (v 25). This is

a promise—if the people will trust God by obeying him, they will find he "heals" them (in the sense of them not experiencing his judgment, v 26), just as he healed the water (v 25).

- **Is Israel's grumbling justified, do you think?** If we focus (as they did) only on the lack of water, grumbling seems fairly justified. But remember, it is only three days since the Israelites have been rescued from Egyptian slavery in the most dramatic fashion as they watched the hand of God parting the Red Sea and defeating the Egyptian army. Then they sang, "The LORD is my strength and my defence … In your unfailing love you will lead the people you have redeemed" (v 2, 13). Now, just 72 hours later, they are thirsty, and they grumble about their lot. When we think of it like this, the Israelites' grumbling is unjustifiable.

3. How is the grumbling in this desert [16 v 1-36] worse than the grumbling at Marah? Now they say that they were better off in Egypt—that the exodus has actually made things worse (v 3). The people are effectively telling God, *We wish you hadn't bothered rescuing us. We wish you'd left us as we were. We were fine in Egypt—it was much better there than here.* **How does God respond?** He generously provides for his ungrateful people. He promises to "rain down bread from heaven for you" (v 4). He provides quail (birds) and then "thin flakes like frost" (v 13-14). Everyone can gather all that they need (v 15-16, 18).

- **Is Israel's grumbling justified, do you think?** It is not only unjustified; it is inexcusable. They question God's character and intentions. One of the characteristics of grumbling is that it often relies on idealised and unrealistic alternatives. In chapter 2, the people were groaning and crying out. Now, all of a sudden they think of Egypt as a wonderful place to live! The Egyptians slave drivers are forgotten. Indeed they suggest it was God who oppressed them in Egypt ("if only we had died by the LORD's hand in Egypt", 16 v 3). And they claim God's intentions are malign ("you have brought us out … to starve this entire assembly").

4. God only gives enough for today, and not for tomorrow as well. In what way is this designed to cause the Israelites to trust him? By only giving enough for each day, God requires his people to trust that he will give them what they need for today, and then again for tomorrow, and then again for the day after. He is teaching them to trust him one day at a time. With the manna, there is to be no alternative but to trust that God will provide tomorrow.

- **God instructs the people to gather double the day before the Sabbath, and nothing on the Sabbath. In what way is this designed to cause the Israelites to trust him?** God calls his people to rest one day a week to rely on his provision, rather than on their own efforts. In telling them both not to collect for tomorrow, and then one day a week to collect enough for tomorrow but then to rest for a day, God is asking his people to trust him in how and what he provides.

- **What does Israel's response show about their view of God (v 19-20, 23-27)?** This is a hard lesson for the Israelites to pay attention to (v 20). Some people gathered more than they needed and "kept part of it until morning". They trust their efforts, their savings and their provision. They do not really trust God to keep providing for them in the future, so

they trust their work today, and they go to bed looking at the pot of manna saved for tomorrow, and that makes them feel secure. But the next morning, it is full of maggots and has started to smell. Again, in v 23-27 their failure to rest shows a lack of trust in God. In going out on the Sabbath to gather more, they show that they are not satisfied with what God has given, and/or that they are not trusting him to keep giving it. **What does this view look like in our time and culture?** Any way in which we trust our own efforts or our own savings to give us satisfaction or security is a way in which we are living as Israel did here. One way to detect this attitude in ourselves or others is to ask, *Can I rest?* If you can't rest—if you're always busy with your work or your family or your ministry—it is because you're not trusting God. You're trying to secure your own future or create your own identity or provide your own justification. You can make excuses, but that's all they are—excuses.

5. How is this episode [in 17 v 1-7] similar to the previous two? Again, they grumble against Moses, demand water and want to return to Egypt (v 1-3). And again, God responds patiently by providing water for them (v 6).

- **When the people grumble against Moses, how are they treating God (v 7)?** They are testing God (v 7)—putting God in the dock and finding him guilty of failing to deliver the life they want. To grumble about what God has (or has not) given us is to "test" his goodness by telling him, *I deserve and need more than you are giving me, and if you don't give me more, I will know you are not good.* When we grumble, we are judging God.

It is important that your group grasp the spiritual seriousness of grumbling here, though it will be picked up on again in Q7 (and reinforced in the Explore More if you have time to cover it).

6. Draw the layout of the scene described in v 5-6. Something like this…

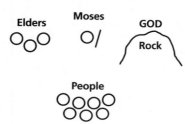

7. Who should be struck by God's judgment? The Israelites. Even now, on the eastern shore, they are still failing to trust and obey God. And they are even accusing God of having murderous intentions towards them. They deserve judgment. **Who is struck, and with what result?** The rock—the rock where God is standing (v 6). Don't miss what a surprising and dramatic moment this is. We would expect God to say in v 6, "Strike the… Israelites"—instead he says, "Strike the… rock". God takes the judgment that his people deserve—and as a result, blessing flows to the people, as the water comes out from the rock to quench the people's thirst.

• **Read 1 Corinthians 10 v 4. In what sense is Christ our "rock"?** What happened at Massah was a picture of, and a pointer to, the cross. At the cross, the great court case between God and humanity came to its climax. On one side was guilty humanity, deserving condemnation. On the other side was the perfect, sinless Son of God, Christ the

Rock. And God the Father said, "Strike the rock". The rod of his judgment fell on Jesus. He is the Rock who bears our judgment.

As a result, blessing flows to God's people. Read John 7 v 38-39 to your group; water flows from God to his people, though this water is symbolic—"by this he meant the Spirit". Through Christ's death, his Spirit flows to his people, bringing his presence. Our spiritual thirst is quenched, eternally, as our guilt is removed at the cross.

EXPLORE MORE
Read Psalm 95 … What was the grumbling a sign of (v 8)? Hardened hearts. We have come across this condition before in Exodus—in Pharaoh. Israel's grumbling is a sign that they do not truly recognise the authority, or trust the goodness, of God.
What were the people doing when they grumbled about God's plan and provision (v 9)? "They tried me"—they put God in the dock, judged him, and found him wanting, even "though they had seen what I did" both at the Red Sea and in the giving of the manna.
What did it lead to (v 10-11)? Judgment. God was angry with them, and they were not able to enter his "rest"—that is, the promised land.
How does this psalm show the link between grumbling, sin, unbelief and judgment? Grumbling is sin because it is judging God: setting ourselves up as able to give a verdict on his actions (and even his character). It is a sign of a hardening, or even hardened, heart. It is a symptom of unbelief. And therefore it deserves, and brings, judgment, if it is not repented of.
What should we do instead of grumbling (v 1-2, 6-7)?
• v 1-2: We should sing with thankful joy

to the LORD (just as Israel had, briefly, in Exodus 15), because he is our Rock—the one who bears the judgment we deserve.

• v 6-7: We should worship and obey God, trusting him to care for and provide for his flock.

8. APPLY: Why is grumbling spiritually serious? (This is an opportunity to underline your answers to the subquestion to Q5, particularly if you have not covered the Explore More section above.) It is putting God "in the dock" and finding him guilty of being ungenerous or uncaring. It is indicative of a hardening heart, and an encouragement to others to harden theirs. So ultimately it is a sign of a lack of trust in God, and therefore brings judgment. **As a congregation, do you tend to help each other stop doing it, or help each other keep doing it? How?** Grumbling grows because it spreads to others. It's infectious. Think how those grumbling conversations unfold. We spread discontent. We reinforce one another's grumbles. This is why it's so important to cut it off at the root. We need to challenge one another when we grumble. We need to say, "Stop. Don't talk to me about it. Go and talk to the person concerned, or go and talk to God, since he's sent the circumstance about which you are concerned." None of us are immune to the contagion—someone else's grumbling gives us all the excuse our hearts need to indulge in it ourselves. But often we let each other's grumbling go unchallenged, or even promote it.

9. APPLY: Read Romans 8 v 28-32. What is the Christian antidote to grumbling given in these verses? God is working everything for our good as we love him (v 28). And the good he is working for us is to make us more like his Son (v 30). How do

we know that he truly wants our good, and will give us what we truly need? He gave us his Son (v 32). He has not withheld anything good from us, and he will not withhold anything necessary for us. He could not have given us anything more, or anything better. So when circumstances are not what we would choose—and perhaps are very, very hard—we can see it as something that our trustworthy, generous God is giving in order to conform us to Christ and bring us to his kingdom eternally. We can trust him to know what he is doing and we can rely on his provision; and so we can (and must) live in gratitude rather than grumbling. We do that as we look at the cross and think, "He is enough. He has provided, and he will provide."

10. How do the Amalekites react to Israel's appearance (v 8)? They attack the Israelites. **What does Moses know is really going on behind their decision (v 15-16)?** By opposing Israel, it was God they were fighting. Their "hands were lifted up against the throne of the LORD".

• **What is the result for the Amalekites (v 13-16)?** They are defeated in battle (notice that the hands of God's servant, Moses, are lifted against them because they lifted their hands against God, v 11-12, 16). And not only that, but they now face God's ongoing, total judgment—they will face God's enmity generation by generation, and eventually be blotted out (v 14).

Note: God goes on lifting his hand against the Amalekites because they go on lifting their hands against him and his people— they attack Israel again a year later (Numbers 14 v 45); they oppose God's people in the promised land (e.g. Judges 3 v 13; 1 Samuel 15 v 1-8); and when God's people are living in exile, Haman the Agagite (named after the Amalekite King Agag, he is almost certainly an Amalekite) seeks to wipe out the Jews (Esther 3 – 10).

11. How does Jethro react to Israel's rescue (18 v 9-11)? He is "delighted" (v 9), and praises the LORD for rescuing Israel (v 10), acknowledging that "the LORD is greater than all other gods" (v 11).

• **What do the Israelites and this Midianite do together (v 12)?** Having made a sacrifice, they join together to eat a meal in the presence of God.

12. Read Matthew 26 v 26-29. What did Jesus encourage his disciples to look forward to as they shared this Passover meal (v 29)? Drinking with him in his Father's kingdom (v 29), beyond his death, which secures their forgiveness (v 28). His greater exodus at the cross and empty tomb (see previous study) will lead to the greater climax of them eating together in his presence at the eternal banquet in his Father's kingdom. And whenever we eat this meal in remembrance of his death, we also look forward to being in his presence and eating with him.

⊗

• **Read 1 Corinthians 10 v 17. What does Paul encourage us to look around at as we share this meal?** Each other! As we share bread and wine, the differences between us are redeemed. Division becomes diversity as we're united in Christ—"we, who are many, are one body, for we all share the one loaf". Christ's sacrifice brings us together and the fruit of that sacrifice is a meal in the presence of God.

• **How is the meal of Exodus 18 v 12**

replicated whenever we share the Lord's Supper together in church? Jethro did not experience the plagues and parting of the Red Sea. But he did experience and share in what they made possible—eating together in the presence of God. So with us—we were not at the foot of the cross, nor did we see the empty tomb, but we do enjoy what they made possible—a meal in the presence of God to which the nations are invited.

13. APPLY: Do you (individually and as a church) tend to view "the nations":
• **with suspicion, assuming they will hate you and need to be kept at arm's length?**
• **with optimism, ensuring that you avoid your local community criticising or hating you in any way?**
• **with surprise, because the community does not seem to welcome your church's presence?**
How does Exodus 17 v 8 – 18 v 27 both reshape your expectations and challenge your behaviour? Jethro reminds us that some from the nations will be glad at what God has done, and will celebrate his deliverance, joining his people to eat with them. (And, of course, our own stories should tell us this too—if you are not a Jew, then you are from "the nations", brought into God's people because the nations are invited in).

The Amalekites remind us that the nations will not necessarily welcome the presence of God's people, and that simply by belonging to God, we will be hated by the world sometimes. The criticism or even hatred of our community is not something to be avoided at all costs, nor something to be surprised about.

So our expectation should be that we will be

opposed by those who are not part of God's people, but also and at the same time, that some will join us. We are to be welcoming and open to those whom God brings into to his people, while at the same time resolving to be faithful to God even when that causes us to be opposed by the world.

Exodus 19 – 24

6 YOU SHALL...

THE BIG IDEA
We obey God's will because we are the rescued people of the holy, pure God, tasked with showing his goodness to his world. His will is expressed in his law, which also shows us our need for salvation and the perfection of Christ.

SUMMARY
Note: This is a very long study, covering five chapters and some complex ideas. If you are able to, you could split it into two, breaking the study after Q6 and including the two Explore More sections.

- Israel arrives at Mount Sinai to worship God, just as he had promised Moses in 3 v 11-12 (19 v 1-2).
- God describes his people's new identity, and the people commit to their covenant relationship with the LORD (19 v 3-8).
- Israel prepares for the arrival of God (19 v 9-25).
- The Ten Commandments (20 v 1-17).
- The people respond to God's presence with fear (20 v 18-21).
- God continues to give his law (20 v 22 – 23 v 33).
- Israel commits to keep God's law; God invites Israel's elders halfway up the mountain with Moses to enjoy a meal in his presence (24 v 1-12).
- Moses goes up the mountain to receive more instructions from God, and is up there for 40 days (24 v 13-18).

OPTIONAL EXTRA
Play a game of *Strange laws: real or fake?* Get a list of strange laws from the internet, and then write some fake ones of your own. Read them one by one to your group, who have to vote as to whether they think they are real or fake. You could also include some biblical laws.

GUIDANCE FOR QUESTIONS
1. When and why is the rule of law a good thing? When and why is it a negative thing? It's all too easy for us to think of "law" in a negative way. We see it as something restrictive. But a fair, just rule of law is a great blessing in any society. The alternatives are anarchy, in which the strong exploit the weak with impunity; or oppression, in which the rule of law is unjust and tyrannical, and is used for the strong to exploit the weak. We tend to see the rule of law as negative when we don't feel like obeying it, or it inconveniences us, or we disagree with it. But encourage your group to see the rule of law as negative in this larger sense—when it is unjust or tyrannical.

- **How do you feel about obeying God's Old Testament law?** Your group may have varying answers, based on different understandings of the law in the Old Testament. It will help you spot any misunderstandings as to what God's law is, and how it applies to us as Christians today. The final question returns to this issue.

2. Read Exodus 3 v 11-12. What is the huge significance of the details of 19 v 1-2? What do they tell us about God? Don't underestimate the significance of 19 v 1-2—it is the moment God keeps his promise, made to a single man in 3 v 12, to bring out of Egypt a whole people to worship him at Mount Horeb, or Sinai. These verses say, *God always keeps his promises to his people.*

3. What has God done for his people? 19 v 4: He has judged Egypt and he has carried his people "on eagles' wings" out of slavery, so that they might be his people, in relationship with him. **What does God call his people to do in response (v 4-5)?** v 5: "Obey me fully and keep my covenant."

• **How does God describe Israel's identity (v 5-6)? Put each description into your own words.**
1. *God's treasured possession (v 5)*. This phrase is used elsewhere of a king's private treasury (1 Chronicles 29 v 3; Ecclesiastes 2 v 8). Israel are God's treasury. Israel were chosen from the world to be God's valuable people, belonging to and beloved by him.
2. *A kingdom of priests (Exodus 19 v 6)*. Israel were to be a kingdom which, as a whole, had a priestly function similar to the priests in the tabernacle. The priests represented the LORD. The people couldn't go into the Most Holy Place to witness God's glory, but they could see the high priest, who could witness his glory there.

The priests also represented Israel. Aaron's ephod carried stones representing the tribes of Israel (28:6-28). When he stood before God, Israel stood before God—when he presented the blood of the sacrifice which secured forgiveness, Israel presented it and benefited from it.
The priests made relationship with God possible for Israel. In the same way, Israel, as a priestly kingdom, created the possibility of such a relationship. As a priestly kingdom, Israel was to represent God to the world through mission, and represent the world to God through prayer.
3. *A holy nation (v 6)*. They were to be holy as God is holy. In other words, God's people were to reflect God's distinctive character in their distinctive life so that the character of God was displayed to the nations. They were to be a light to the nations.

4. What do the instructions of verses 10-15 and 20-24, and the experiences of v 16-19, show about whether and how God can dwell near people? God tells Moses to "consecrate" the people (v 10). This included washing their clothes and abstaining from sex (v 10-11, 15). The priests must also be consecrated (v 22). And even after all this, God tells Moses that the people and the priests must keep their distance from him, or they will die (v 12-13, 22, 24).
In verses 16-19, as God comes close, the people see lightning and thick cloud, smoke and fire; they hear thunder and a trumpet blast; they feel the mountain trembling. Unsurprisingly, "everyone in the camp trembled" (v 16).
It's as if the holiness of God is nuclear. If you want to approach a nuclear reactor, then you must put on protective clothing,

and even then you must not get too close. In the same way, if the people want to approach God, they must come prepared through consecration, and even then they must not come too close. A nuclear reactor must be encased in layers of concrete. And as the glory of the Lord descends on Mount Sinai, the mountain has three zones of increasing holiness and therefore danger (just as, later, the tabernacle would). Only Moses may ascend to the top. Aaron and the seventy elders may go onto the slopes (v 22). The third zone is the border of the mountain, where the people must remain. Transgressing these boundaries leads to death.

Sinai leaves Israel, and us, in no doubt: God wants a relationship with his people, but God is also dangerously holy.

⌄

• **What is the right response to knowing this is who God is?** Fear (v 16). And then not to be afraid (20 v 20)! This seems contradictory, but Moses is saying, *Don't be afraid, because fear is the right response to God. You're doing the right thing. And this fear will keep you loyal to God.*

5. What has not changed for us, compared with God's people in the time of Exodus? Read 1 Peter 2 v 9-11. Writing to Christians, Peter tells them, "You are a chosen people, a royal priesthood [another way of saying "a kingdom of priests"], a holy nation, God's special possession, that you may declare the praises of him who called you out of darkness into his wonderful light" (1 Peter 2 v 9). This, of course, is the language of Exodus 19. The missional identity which Israel received at Mount Sinai is fulfilled in the church. The church is the people chosen to be a kingdom of priests who make God known to the world. We are the people who declare the praises of God and display his holiness to the nations.

• **What has changed for us? Read Hebrews 12 v 18-24.** God has not changed—he is still nuclear, as it were. People have not changed. We still need to be made holy, or consecrated. But because of Jesus' death in our place—the holy dying for the unholy, giving his holiness—everything has changed, as the writer of Hebrews describes.

We have not come to Mount Sinai. We have come to Mount Zion. Mount Zion is a picture of heaven. The experience of Sinai was full of awe: a mountain burning with fire; the blast of a trumpet that grew louder and louder; the voice of God himself. It was like a volcanic eruption, but with so much more drama. Everyone there was terrified.

But each Sunday we come to something more wonderful. We step into the heavenly gathering. The word "assembly" in Hebrews 12 v 22 means "gathering" or "congregation". By faith, we step into heaven and around us are thousands of angels (v 22) and all the Christians who have died now made perfect (v 23). There are angels standing next to you when you sing. Whenever we gather on earth, we are also simultaneously gathering in heaven. Above all, we gather in the presence of God: "You have come to Mount Zion ... you have come to God." And the mood of this gathering is not fear and terror, but joy.

EXPLORE MORE
Read Hebrews 12 v 25-29. How does the writer link the future of this world to the experience of Israel at Sinai? The

shaking of Mount Sinai will be repeated in the future. At Mount Sinai it was like a localised earthquake—and it was terrifying. Hebrews 12 v 26-27 tells us that a time is coming when not only the earth will shake, but the heavens as well. God is going to come down again; and this time he will shake up the whole of all creation. This is the final day of judgment, when God wraps up history and remakes the world. It will be a day when everyone will assemble before God—and the Bible says it will be a day when people tremble with fear.

With Sinai in our minds' eye, and appreciating that we have been invited to a greater mountain—the heavenly Zion—how should we respond (v 25, 28-29)? V 25: We must take God's voice seriously. We must make very sure that we are not refusing to listen to him. When we gather with God's people to hear God's word, we should do it with seriousness. We are not coming together to be entertained. We are coming to tremble before the holy word of our holy God.

V 28-29: We should be thankful, because if we are trusting in Christ, we are part of a kingdom that cannot be shaken. We stand on a mountain that will stand when God shakes up this world, because we have "come to Mount Zion" (v 22).

How should Exodus 19 and Hebrews affect the way we feel as we get out of bed on Sunday morning and get ready to go to church? When getting out of bed next Sunday (or when our family breakfast has descended into chaos or our church gathering feels dull), remember: we are standing with angels in the presence of God. And so we each participate not as a hassled parent or bored churchgoer, but as a member of the congregation of heaven—the "joyful assembly". Gloom, fear and boredom cannot characterise our attitude to our church. Joy must, and will.

6. APPLY: How does your view of God, and your thinking about dwelling with God, compare with the way he reveals himself in Exodus 19? It is very easy for us to think of God as primarily our friend, or a grandfather in the sky, looking down benevolently even when we sin, making excuses for us. We may even treat him as a genie in a lamp, there for us when we need his help and making no demands on us in terms of how we live or how often we think of him. That is not the God of reality, the God of Exodus 19. He is not a pussycat. He is a lion.

- **How does your view of and commitment to God's people—your church—compare with God's view in Exodus 19 v 5-6?** God rescued each of us to be part of his people. Our church is not an optional extra to our Christian lives. And he rescued us to be part of his church which shows his nature and speaks his truth to the nations. Help your group realise the amazing identity of God's people, of your local church; and the awesome responsibility he has given you. Encourage them to be specific about how they might need to change their thinking and actions. Do they need to stop skipping church to go to sports matches or for a weekend trip? Do they need to stop standing on the periphery? Do they need to stop thinking of church as a refuge from the world, and start thinking of it as a mission to the world?

7. Read Hebrews 8 v 7-13, Romans 7 v 6 and Galatians 6 v 2. What difference does the new covenant make?
Note: The aim here is not to understand everything God says in each of these

passages, but to understand what they say about the difference between the old and new covenants, and the role of the law in each.

Hebrews 8 v 7-13: In the new covenant, the Law of Moses written on tablets of stone is replaced by the law of the Spirit written on our hearts (see also Jeremiah 31 v 31-34).

Romans 7 v 6: We are "released from the law", but we still "serve"—now the Spirit illuminates God's word so that we know God's will and want to keep it.

Galatians 6 v 2: We are now to keep "the law of Christ". It's not the Law of Moses that gives shape to the Christian life, but Jesus. We're called to be Christ-like, and not law-keepers.

Note: Don't allow yourselves to spend too long on this question. Some of the issues it raises are answered in the rest of the study; others are not, but are best wrestled with outside the group time, through further reading. Your group members might want to start with *Exodus For You*, pages 159-182, where I go into greater detail on this.

8. [Read Exodus 20 v 1-21 and Mark 12 v 28-34]. How do the two greatest commandments (Mark 12 v 18-31) lie behind the Ten Commandments in the Law of Moses? It may help your group to print out the Ten Commandments on a sheet for them each to have, so that they can easily look at them and these verses at the same time (and they can use the sheet again for Q9 and 10).

Some of the Ten Commandments reflect both of the "greatest commandments". In one sense, each of numbers 5-10 expresses love for God because in obeying them, we obey him, and each clearly is a way of loving a neighbour. Numbers 1-4 are more focused on our love for God, rather than our

neighbour. But allow your group to come up with differing answers—the point is simply to see that the Ten Commandments reflect God's will for us to love him and love our neighbour.

• **Read Exodus 21 v 28-29. How do the two greatest commandments lie behind this command?** Israelites were to love their neighbours by not holding someone responsible for something that was an accident. Equally, they were to see that they themselves would be responsible for an accident that they could have prevented, so leading them to take steps to prevent injury to their neighbour wherever they could.

And in obeying this command, they were loving God, because they were loving their neighbour, as he commands.

So what timeless lessons are there for us in this command, even if we don't own a bull?!
• I shouldn't blame someone if they accidentally harm me.
• If I can anticipate an accident, then I should take steps to prevent it.

9. Read Romans 3 v 20-22. What does the law do? What does it enable us to appreciate? It makes us conscious of our sin. It shows us God's standards, and when we compare them to our own thoughts, words and deeds, we see that we fall short—that we are sinners. And so we are able to appreciate a way of being made right with God that does not rely on our law-keeping, but is "apart from law".

• **Re-read Exodus 20 v 2-17 as a checklist by which you can assess your life. How does this exercise cause you to appreciate the great truth that in the new covenant, "now apart from the law the righteousness of God has** been made known … righteousness [that] is given through faith in Jesus Christ" (Romans 3 v 21-22)? Because we do not keep the commandments! (**Note:** Jesus extends the applicability of the commands to heart attitudes—I may not be a physical adulterer, but Jesus includes lust as adultery; and I may not be a murderer, but Jesus includes anger in this command—see Matthew 5 v 21-22, 27-28). We are law-breakers, and it is only as we realise the depth and seriousness of our rebellion, and our powerlessness to prevent our own sin, that we appreciate what it is to be made righteous by God, through faith, rather than having to try to make ourselves righteous (or stay righteous), through obedience.

10. Re-read Exodus 20 v 2-17 as a checklist by which you can assess Jesus' life. How does this exercise cause you to appreciate the holiness of Christ? As you consider how Jesus was holy, sinless and pure, in his thoughts and actions, and how he perfectly kept each of these commandments, you may want to pause to pray in praise of this perfectly righteous man.

• **Read Matthew 5 v 17. If the law points us to God's will, and to our need for a Saviour, how does Jesus "fulfil" the law?**
1. By embodying love for God and love for others. Jesus is the epitome of the law—the law in action.
2. By keeping the law as a human. He fulfils the demands of the law.
3. By meeting the need the law exposes. Having kept the law on our behalf, he died as a law-breaker (Galatians 3 v 13), so that we might not face the punishment that our rebellion deserves,

but enjoy the blessing that his law-keeping merits.

EXPLORE MORE
Read Exodus 21 v 12 – 23 v 9. What do all these laws have in common? They are dealing with what happens when someone commits (or plans to commit) a crime. In each case, there is either a demand for the restoration of what has been taken/lost, and/or a punishment equivalent to the harm done (or intended).
How do the penalties differ if:
• **the wrongdoing is accidental?** There's restitution, but no punishment (e.g. 21 v 35, 22 v 6).
• **the wrongdoing is deliberate but only attempted?** There's punishment, but no restitution.
• **the wrongdoing is deliberate and committed?** There's punishment and restitution (e.g. 21 v 29-30).
Our crime against God—our sin—is both deliberate and committed. What punishment is required—and how does Jesus experience it? Death is the punishment (see Romans 6 v 23; 1 v 32). And so the cross is where Jesus took what our deliberate, "successful" crimes deserve.
Read Exodus 21 v 1-11 and 23 v 10-13. What are these laws about? 21 v 1-11 makes provision for slaves to be liberated. 23 v 10-13 makes provision for rest for the land and for workers.

11. What is the climax of this giving of God's law to God's people (24 v 1-2, 9-12)? A meal at which the representatives of Israel eat and drink in the presence of God. They have to stand at a distance, apart from Moses (v 1-2)—but they get to see God and are given a sight of his majesty (v 10-11), and eat and drink there. **How did Moses prepare for this (v 4b-8)?** He…

- organised sacrifices to be made on behalf of the people (v 4-6).
- read God's covenant laws to the people so that they could commit to being his obedient covenant people (v 7).
- confirmed that the blood of the sacrifices had made his covenant people holy (this is what the sprinkling represents, v 8).

- **Read Luke 22 v 14-20. How are we, once again, being pointed to the awesome and exciting nature of the Lord's Supper?**
  - Jesus is our sacrifice—he sacrifices himself on behalf of his people, so that we can approach and enjoy the presence of God.
  - Jesus is the one who has obeyed the law perfectly for us.
  - Jesus' blood is what confirms the new covenant—we are made holy by him.
  - We eat and drink in his spiritual presence now, knowing that one day we will be invited into the very presence of God in his kingdom, to eat and drink. We will not have to stand at a distance!

12. APPLY: How have these chapters:
- **enlarged your view of God?**
- **increased your appreciation of Jesus Christ?**
- **reshaped your view of God's law in your life?**

This is an opportunity to reflect and sum up all that your group have seen in Exodus 19 – 24. You might like to ask each member to spend a few minutes reflecting and writing their answers individually, before sharing them with the group.

One helpful way to shape our approach to, and application of, God's Old Testament law as Christians is to ask when we read a portion of it:

1. how does this law express love for God or love for neighbour? How might the same principles be expressed today?
2. how does this law expose my sinfulness and need?
3. how did Christ perfectly keep this law or the principles it embodies?
4. does this law picture his work of salvation in some way?

7 Exodus 32 – 34
THE GOLDEN CALF: TRAGEDY AND MERCY

THE BIG IDEA
Sin is idolatry, which is spiritual adultery against the God who has rescued, cared for and committed himself to us. The glory of God is that he punishes our sin, and yet he also has mercy on his people, because Christ died on our behalf—so as we gaze at Christ, we see his glory, are transformed by his glory, and are motivated to live uncompromising lives of loving obedience.

SUMMARY
This study moves forwards to chapters 32 – 34, which record what Israel did at the foot of the mountain while Moses was at the top. We will return to chapters 25 – 31 (which contain instructions for the building of the tabernacle, where God would dwell among his people) in the next study.
- The people, including Aaron, worship a golden calf instead of/as well as the LORD (32 v 1-6).
- God decides to destroy his unfaithful people; Moses speaks for them and God has mercy (32 v 7-14).
- Moses returns to the camp; partial judgment comes as 3,000 are killed (32 v 15-30).
- Moses speaks to God and begs God not only to forgive and remain with him, but with the whole people, despite their sin; God agrees (32 v 31 – 33 v 17).
- God shows Moses his glory by enabling him to hear a description of his character as he passes Moses by (33 v 18 – 34 v 9).
- The covenant is repeated and laws are put in place to help Israel live as God's people

(34 v 10-28).
- Moses goes on meeting with and hearing from God in the tent of meeting—this taste of God's glory makes his face radiant (34 v 29-35).

OPTIONAL EXTRA
Give each member of the group a lump of playdough or similar modelling clay, and have a competition to see who can sculpt the best cow in a short time limit. Keep the models on display during the study and refer to them during Q3 and Q6 to highlight the ridiculousness of worshipping created things.

GUIDANCE FOR QUESTIONS
1. When is compromise dangerous, or inexcusable? Compromise is usually seen as a positive—and, in many situations, it is necessary and a sign of wisdom and maturity. But this question encourages your group to think about when it is not. They may come up with personal examples of negative compromise, or more national-level ideas. British appeasement of German expansionism in the 1930s is arguably a good example of dangerous compromise; a husband deciding to settle on a compromise between his wedding vows and his attraction to other women by taking a mistress is inexcusable.

- **In those situations, why is compromise often still attractive?** Often, we feel tension between what we ought to do, and what we want to do. Since we're sinful, this is often a tension between

doing right and wrong. Compromise on what we know is right is attractive. In many situations, we settle for somewhere between the right thing and the worst thing, so that we can still feel we're not "totally" wrong, and can excuse what we're doing, feeling that we're justified. A husband who looks at pornography and excuses his actions because it's not a real affair is finding a compromise between what he ought to do, and the worst he could do (and may feel like doing).
As you'll see together, this is what Israel do with the golden calf. You could return to these questions after Q6 and/or Q12.

2. [In Exodus 32 v 1-6] What do the people do? They ask Aaron (Moses' brother) to make them "gods who will go before us" (v 1), and then give Aaron their jewellery so he can make "an idol cast in the shape of a calf" (v 3-4). They then worship the calf as their god/gods "who brought you up out of Egypt" (v 4), and present offerings to it, holding a feast and indulging in "revelry" (a word which implies an orgy—v 6). **Why?** Because "they saw that Moses was so long in coming down from the mountain" (v 1). In fact, he had only been gone 40 days.

- **What does Aaron do?** When the people demand that he makes them "gods who will go before us", he tells them to give him their jewellery (v 2), makes them "an idol cast in the shape of a calf" (v 4), and, having built an altar in front of the calf, announces that "there will be a festival to the LORD" (v 5) that is centred on worshipping the calf. **Why?** It seems Aaron is responding to the people with a compromise ("gathered round Aaron" in v 1 has the sense of coming to oppose or pressure him). Verse 4 could read, "This is your God". So he may well be attempting to find a compromise between the people's wish for a different god, and the right course of action, which is unswerving loyalty to the LORD.

3. What do you make of the decision of the people, and of Aaron? God introduced the Ten Commandments by reminding the people that he had rescued them from slavery in Egypt (20 v 2). Now Aaron uses the same language—but about the golden calf (32 v 4). The people want gods "who will go before us" (v 1)—but this is exactly what the Lord had done (14 v 19; 23 v 23). The people are robbing God of his glory, exchanging it for a lifeless lump of shiny metal.
Refer your group to the Ten Commandments. The people appear to want to break the first commandment—to replace God with a different god. Aaron's compromise solution requires breaking the second commandment (no idols) in order to not break the first (no other gods).
What does it reveal about them? Israel has been rescued by God to be his people, the beginning of a new humanity to live in his promised, good land—a glimpse of life as it was designed to be. Israel has been called to be a kingdom of priests, displaying and declaring God to the world. But the old humanity lurks in the heart of the new humanity. The people are sinners.

- **How is Aaron's conduct here a particular warning to church leaders, do you think?** With Moses (and Joshua) up the mountain, Aaron is the leader of God's people. And he leads them into compromised idolatrous worship. He is not the initiator of this—but he capitulates to the people and so he is complicit in this. *I will lead you… wherever you want to go*, he says in effect. And that is not leadership; it is cowardice. It is not loving; it is selfish. Leaders must resist the pressures of the culture if they are to lead God's people in true worship of the true God, the only God who can and will "go before us".

• **Read Psalm 106 v 19-22 and Romans 1 v 25. What did God's people make of it, generations later?** *Psalm 106 v 20:* It was a stupid lack of memory and loss of perspective. The people forgot the God who had saved them, and instead worshipped an inanimate "idol cast from metal" made in the "image of a bull". The writer of the psalm adds, in case we'd missed the point, "which eats grass". The people rejected the God of everything, who keeps his promises, for a lump of metal shaped like something that eats grass. That is stupid.
Romans 1 v 25: It was a horrendous exchange. Paul seems to have this episode in mind as he talks about humans exchanging the truth of God for a lie, in ceasing to worship and thank the real God as instead "they worshipped and served created things rather than the Creator' (v 25).

• **Read James 4 v 4. How is this a good description of Israel in Exodus 32?** James says that those who live in friendship with the world are in "enmity against God", and, perhaps even more searingly, are "adulterous people". And this is what Israel does—the choice of the idol-shape was not arbitrary; a bull was a common symbol of strength and fertility in surrounding nations. It is a sign of "friendship" with the world rather than fidelity to God. It is idolatry, and James

says that idolatry is spiritual adultery. In Exodus 24, the people had entered into a covenant with God. God had become their husband. They had made covenant vows that were not unlike wedding vows: "When Moses went and told the people all the Lᴏʀᴅ's words and laws, they responded with one voice, 'Everything the Lᴏʀᴅ has said we will do'" (24 v 3). Now, in chapter 32, it is as if a husband has found his wife in bed with another man while they are still on their honeymoon.

4. Why does God not destroy his idolatrous, adulterous people (32 v 7-14, 30-34)? Verses 7-10 sound like the end of the story for Israel. God has "seen these people" (v 9) and what they have done— they are "a stiff-necked people" who will not bow their heads to their Creator and Rescuer. So the Creator will de-create (v 10). Only one man is not part of this great sinful compromise, Moses: and God announces that he will bring his promises to fulfilment through this single Israelite: "I will make you into a great nation" (v 10).
Then Moses intervenes, praying on behalf of the people. He does not leave the people alone to face their fate. Instead, he pleads for them. Notice his reasoning is on the basis of God's glory:
• v 11-12: Destroying Israel will damage God's reputation.
• v 13: Destroying Israel will break God's promises.
• v 14: God hears the prayers of Moses and relents.
In v 30, Moses thinks he might be able to "make atonement for [their] sin". What he has in mind becomes clearer in v 31-32— he acknowledges that the Israelites have forfeited their right to be in God's "book of life" (see Psalm 69 v 28; Revelation 20 v 12-15). But he offers to substitute himself

for them, to be blotted out instead (Exodus 32 v 32). But God says that he cannot (v 33). Judgment will come (and it comes in part through the plague in v 35). Full judgment is postponed due to Moses' intervention. But make sure the group notice that it has not been cancelled.

5. How do the events of verses 15-30 show the seriousness of idolatry?

- v 15-16, 19: Moses smashes the stone tablets that "were the work of God" and had written the "covenant law" on them. It is a sign that Israel's idolatry has broken the covenant between themselves and God. It is like a husband finding his wife in bed with someone else on his honeymoon, and throwing down his wedding ring to show the seriousness of what she has done to their relationship.
- v 20: Moses destroys the idol and makes the people drink the remains. He is wanting to show the idiocy of their idol-worship—they are worshipping something that is effectively excrement. It is the opposite of eternal. He wants the people to see the ridiculousness of their exchange and their compromise.
- v 25-29: The people are running wild (v 6, 18-19) and so he calls them either to choose to side with God, or to stay siding with the world. He wants them to recognise the depth of their sin. It has to be stopped. This is why he and the Levites kill 3,000 people. They are running wild, and they need to be stopped. This passage makes uncomfortable reading for us. It seems so brutal. But sin is brutal. This story reveals the deadly seriousness of sin. Temptation presents sin as attractive and harmless. But in reality sin looks like 3,000 rotting corpses. Death is sin made visible.
- v 30: Idolatry is a "great sin" and it severs relationship with God. It requires atoning

for, and atonement cannot be assumed because it is not automatic.

6. APPLY: What are the "golden calves" that we are attracted to? Why are they harder to spot in our own culture than in other cultures? Remember what Israel are doing: they let the nations set the agenda. They want a god who is visible and manageable. Even if they are not replacing God, they are reducing him.

It is the same today. But it is harder to spot because we are so used to the ways in which God is re-cast and reduced, or to the alternative gods that people choose to worship, that we don't spot them. Some people want the benefits of being part of the church, but they do not want to relate to God on his terms. Or they want the blessings of God along with the pleasures of indulgence. They want forgiveness from God, but they do not want to obey his will. Some people want to pick and choose which bits of the Bible they accept. Naturally, we all re-mould God in our image or our culture's image, rather than remembering that we are made in his image.

And as Christians, we worry that if we do not compromise, then our culture will not respect us. But the world will not respect us any more if we change with every cultural fashion. And if we become no different to the surrounding culture, then we have nothing distinctive or worthwhile to say. If we simply echo the world, then we offer no alternative. The world has plenty of temples to its idols; there is no call or excuse for making God's church into another one.

- **How does Exodus 32 show us:**
  - **the different ways in which we might compromise in our relationship with God?**
  - **the dangers of doing this?**

• the inexcusability of doing this?
This question is designed to underline the seriousness of sin, including compromise. You could refer back to Q1 here.

7. What will God do for the people and what won't he do (33 v 1-6)?

• v 1-3a: God says he will fulfil his promise to Abraham by giving the Israelites the land of Canaan.

• v 3b, 5: God will not go with them, because if he does, he may destroy them due to their "stiff-necked" sinfulness.

Note: The reason the people are told to remove their ornaments (v 5) is probably because these were what they had used to create the calf in 32 v 2-3. So it is an appropriate sign of repentance.

• **How do verses 7-11 show why the people "began to mourn" (v 4) when they heard what God had said?** At first sight, v 1-3 looks like a good deal. God will give the people the promised land, but without the threat of his perfect, holy presence. All God's blessings, without God. But the people don't think it is a good deal (v 4). Verses 7-11 give a sense of what's being lost. God meets with his people (v 7-8). His presence is symbolised by the pillar of cloud, which has led and protected them. The Lord spoke to Moses, the leader of the people, "as one speaks to a friend" (v 11). God has been among his people as a friend—now he is their enemy.

8. What is amazing about Moses' response in verses 15-16 to God's promise to him in verse 14? God has just assured Moses that he will be with him, and Moses will enjoy "rest"—life as it was designed to be enjoyed. But this is not enough for Moses. He turns down God's

blessing and presence if it's for him alone. He comes before the God who says, "I might destroy you", not to plead his own case or point out that he has not sinned as the people have, but rather, to argue for God's presence to go with all of them.

• **What does it tell us Moses cares about most?** His only aim is the ongoing presence of God among the people of God. He cares more about that than God's blessings for them. And he cares more about them than he does himself. For all his faults, this is what makes Moses one of the great men of history.

9. So what is the glory of God (34 v 5-7)? It is his character (because "name" represents someone's character). The glory of God is his mercy and compassion, his love and forgiveness; and his justice in punishing the guilty. His glory is that he is the God who burns with anger, but is also the God who is slow to anger; the God who does not ignore sin, but who also forgives sin.

10. Read John 1 v 17 and Romans 3 v 25-26. How is the tension in the glory revealed to Moses resolved by the life and death of Jesus? Because in Jesus, grace and truth arrived—forgiveness and punishment, mercy and justice, grace and truth meet in Jesus. And when God "presented Christ as a sacrifice of atonement" (Romans 3 v 25)—when Jesus died as a sacrifice for our sins—God demonstrated his righteousness, his glory, because at the cross the truth of sin was recognised, punished and accounted for—God was "just"—but at the same time God's rebellious people were forgiven so that we can be loved and blessed. The resolution of the tension in the "glory" of God is the cross.

EXPLORE MORE
... Read Exodus 34 v 8-28. How would the laws mentioned in each of these sections help?

- **v 11-12:** Political treaties with other nations will lead to compromise with other nations, and a reliance on other nations rather than on God.
- **v 13-15:** Clearly, joining the religious practices of other nations will pull Israel away from worshipping God alone.
- **v 16:** Since your marriage partner has a huge influence over your affections and decisions, to marry someone who worships a different god cannot be wise for people who already struggle to worship the true God.
- **v 18-26:** These verses are a reminder of the key festivals in the Israelite calendar, which commemorate identity-forming events, helping the people to remember:
  - the Passover in the Festival of Unleavened Bread (v 18).
  - their redemption from Egypt in the ongoing redemption of their firstborn (v 19-20).
  - the rest God has given them from oppression as they keep the Sabbath (v 21).
  - God's provision as they celebrate the Festival of Weeks (v 22-23, 26).

What do you think these laws reveal about the will of God for his people, on which we need to base our decisions as his people today? In the last study, we saw that God's old-covenant laws are not binding for Christians today, but we are to discern what God's timeless will is that underlies the laws, and obey God by applying his will to our lives. So for instance, while we may marry someone who is not an Israelite (v 16), God's timeless will is that we do not marry someone who is not a worshipper of the true God, through Christ; or who will not help us to worship him alone.

11. [In 34 v 29-35] What effect does "seeing" God's glory, through hearing God's words on the mountain and in "the Lᴏʀᴅ's presence" in the tabernacle, have on Moses? His face is radiant—he is transformed by seeing God's glory.

- **Read John 1 v 14, 18; 2 Corinthians 3 v 7-8, 18. Who can be transformed by the Lᴏʀᴅ's presence today?** *John 1:* We can, if we know Jesus and experience the grace and truth, the glory of God, that we find in him. In Exodus 34, it is only Moses who enjoys the transforming radiance of seeing God's glory. Now, it is everyone who knows Jesus Christ. **How?** 2 Corinthians 3: By "the ministry of the Spirit" (v 8), which is even more "glorious" than what Moses experienced. What does the Spirit do? He shows us Jesus as we "contemplate the Lord's glory" (v 18), and transforms us into his image as we do that. Just as Moses heard God's glory (rather than seeing it) both on the mountain and in the tabernacle, so we hear God's glory each time we hear the story of Jesus. So we are transformed by God's glorious presence as we read the Bible, hear the word preached, sing the word, encourage others with the gospel and so on, because through all this the Spirit shows us Jesus. He is a transforming vision.

12. APPLY: What might it look like for you to be transformed by seeing the glory of God in Christ this week? Encourage your group to think about the various ways they can hear of, or "see", Jesus. And encourage them to approach regular disciplines such as their "quiet time", or singing in church gatherings, with excitement, and to ask the Spirit to show them Jesus and his glory as they do it. Sometimes our problem is not that we do not read our Bible, listen to sermons etc. but we do these things drily, without asking and expecting the Spirit to show us God's glory as we do them.

• **How can we use this glimpse of the glory of God in Exodus 34, and the greater sight of the glory of God in Jesus, to undermine the attraction of compromise?** This question brings the two halves of the study together. Encourage your group to see the battle against compromise with idolatry not only in negative terms ("I must try not to do that because it's spiritual adultery") but in positive ones ("Why would I want to worship anything other than my glorious Lord Jesus?"). It is as we appreciate the glory of God in the person of Christ that the lure of our golden calves is extinguished.

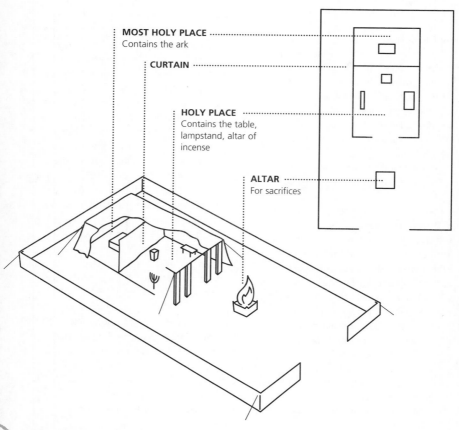

MOST HOLY PLACE
Contains the ark

CURTAIN

HOLY PLACE
Contains the table, lampstand, altar of incense

ALTAR
For sacrifices

8 Exodus 25 – 31; 35 – 40
AT HOME WITH GOD

THE BIG IDEA
The tabernacle was the place where God lived with his people, and where he showed them what life in his home was like—the role that the church now plays today as we look forward to eternity in God's presence.

SUMMARY
- God instructs Moses on how to build the tabernacle (see diagram on previous page, in which he will dwell among his people (25 v 1 – 27 v 21).
- Instructions for how the priests who work in the tabernacle are to be dressed, and how they must prepare for their duties (28 v 1 – 29 v 46).
- More instructions about the items that will go in the tabernacle (30 v 1-38).
- God appoints and enables craftsmen to work on the tabernacle and gives instructions for resting on the Sabbath (31 v 1-18).
- Moses passes on the tabernacle instructions to the people; the tabernacle is constructed (35 v 1 – 38 v 31).
- The priests are prepared to do their work (39 v 1-31).
- Moses inspects the tabernacle and finishes the work (39 v 32 – 40 v 33).
- God's glory—his presence—fills the tabernacle (40 v 34-38).

OPTIONAL EXTRA
Ask group members to bring with them a couple of photographs of items/furniture in their house that other group members may not have noticed or recognise if they have visited them. Take all the photos, and mix them up. Ask the group to identify whose house is whose, based on the photos of the items/furniture. Obviously, members have to stay quiet when their own house contents are being shown! The point is that, usually, what someone puts on display in their house says something about what they are like, what they have done, what is important to them, and so on. God's "home"—the tabernacle—is, as you will see, no different.

GUIDANCE FOR QUESTIONS
1. When someone walks into your living room, what impression of you and your life do your fixtures and fittings give? This does not need to be a long (or overly self-critical!) discussion—you could link back to it as you answer Q6.

2. What do the Israelites need to offer to God, and what are these offerings for (25 v 1-9)? The offerings are listed in v 3-7—precious metals and stones, fine embroidery materials, skins and leathers— the best the people have. They are all to be used to "make a sanctuary for me" (v 8)—a "tabernacle" with all its furnishings (v 9).

- **What is exciting about verse 8?** "I will dwell among them." In this sanctuary, God will live. Moses had encountered the presence of God in Exodus 3, and the people had seen the presence of God at the top of Mount Sinai in Exodus 19 – 20. But now, God will come to live among his people.

3. Fill in the table to see how God's tabernacle is a picture of the Garden of Eden. See table on next page.

Genesis	Exodus	The link
2 v 12	25 v 3-7	The materials used (notice the repetition of gold and onyx
2 v 9	25 v 31-39	The lampstand's design details are tree-like
1 v 3, 6, 9, 14, 20, 24, 26	25 v 1; 30 v 11, 17, 22, 34; 31 v 1, 12	And God said/the Lord said
2 v 1-3	31 v 12-17	Sabbath rest is the climax of both accounts
2 v 21-22; 3 v 8	25 v 8	God is present

4. What does the furniture in the tabernacle tell us about God and his home?

- **The ark, 25 v 10-22, especially v 16, 22. (Hint: The ark has the same proportions as the footstool of an ancient king.)** Israel's king is God. He reigns from heaven; seated there with the ark as his footstool on earth. This is the point where God's throne in heaven touches the earth (see 1 Samuel 4 v 4; 2 Samuel 6 v 2). In the ark is the covenant law. God will rule his people through his law—so (v 22) here he will "meet with you". In God's home, he reigns and gives life through his rule of love.

- **The table (25 v 23-30):** This is a meal-table, laid up and ready to be sat round. God is inviting his people to eat with him, to live as his family and share food and fellowship at his table.

- **The lampstand (25 v 31-40—Hint: Read Psalm 119 v 105 and think about what a light does.)** A light guides the way. God's home is a place of guidance, of truth and clarity.

5. [Read Exodus 26 v 31-37] What is to be woven onto this curtain? Cherubim (v 31)—angels. These are not small infants, as in popular imagination, but God's warrior-messengers. **Where is it to be hung?** With the ark (the place where God will meet with his people) behind it (v 33), so that "the curtain will separate the Holy Place from the Most Holy Place (see diagram on p 104).

- **Read Genesis 3 v 24. What is significant about the picture of the cherubim on the curtain, and its placement in the temple?** The cherubim in Genesis 3 were placed on the edge of Eden after the first humans sinned, to guard the way back to God. They were a sign of humanity's exile from home, and a sign that there was no way back. Embodied in the architecture of the tabernacle was this symbol of God's inaccessibility. As you stood before the curtain, on your right was "the bread of the Presence" and on your left was the lampstand, both promising relationship with God. But in front of you was the curtain preventing a relationship with God. It hung there to protect you from God, because sinful people cannot survive an encounter with the holy God. As you stood before the curtain, home was so close and so far away. The tabernacle was so full of promise and so full of danger.

6. Read John 14 v 2-3. Jesus is talking the night before he died. How does the tabernacle layout and furniture help us to appreciate the wonder of his promise

here? Jesus was saying that he was going to prepare a place for his people in God's "house", and that one day "you also may be where I am". Take time to appreciate what Jesus was promising—that his death and resurrection, ascension and return would mean that humans would be brought into God's presence, his home, to enjoy life with him for ever. Jesus is the way home.

- **Read Matthew 27 v 50-51. What did Jesus' death achieve?**
  Note: Once God's people were settled in the promised land, living in permanent homes, God told Solomon to build him a permanent home too—so the tabernacle was replaced by the temple.
  As Jesus died, the temple curtain was torn in two—his death radically rearranged the layout of the temple. Now the way home to God was open.

7. APPLY: What difference would it make if you were more assured of, and more excited about, your eternal home? Think about how we would react both to disasters and triumphs; to things that bore us or disappoint us, and to things we really look forward to. And think about how we would react to our sinfulness. We would be more joyful, more confident, more able to stay calm in difficult circumstances, more able to deal with disappointment without feeling despair, and more determined to invite others "home".
If you have time, read Hebrews 10 v 19-22 and spend time praying together in light of the great truth that in Jesus, the way home is open.

EXPLORE MORE
What must [the priests] wear (28 v 4)?
A breastplate, an ephod, a robe, a woven tunic, a turban and a sash.

What is the significance of the ephod and breastplate (v 12, 17-21, 29-30)?
Ephod: The names of the twelve tribes of Israel are inscribed on the ephod. So when the priest comes "before the Lord" (v 12), in a sense every Israelite is there.
Breastplate: This is tied to the front of the priest over the ephod (v 22-28). Sown into it are twelve precious stones (v 17-21), which again represent the twelve tribes of Israel. Again, the point is that when the priest, Aaron, enters the presence of the Lord, the whole of Israel does (v 30).
Also, in the breastpiece rest "the Urim and the Thummim" (v 30). We don't really know what these were except that they were used for making decisions. They probably involved different coloured stones which were selected at random to determine God's will. The point is that this was the means by which God showed his people his will for them (v 30).
What does this tell us about the role of the priest? He represents the people before God. It's as if he carries them into God's presence, where (as we have seen) they cannot go by themselves. And he represents God to the people, by using the Urim and Thummim to reveal God's will, "making decisions for the Israelites" (v 30).
How are the priests prepared for their duties (29 v 1-4, 10-28)? Through washing and sacrifice. Priests, like the rest of the people, are sinful human beings. So to be "consecrated" (v 1)—made fit for God's presence—the priests must be symbolically washed clean and they need to lay their hands on the animals to be sacrificed (v 10, 15, 19) to symbolically transfer their sin to the animal that then dies for it.
What will the work of the priests enable them to do (v 42-46)? *Offer the "burnt offering"*—a sin-bearing sacrifice made on behalf of the people (v 42).

Meet with God and hear from him (v 42)—and through the priests, the Israelites will also meet with God (v 43).

Because sacrifices for sins are being made by the priests, God will be able to continue dwelling among the Israelites (v 45). Ultimately, all this is aimed at maintaining ongoing relationship with and worship of the God who has rescued his people (v 46).

Read Hebrews 9 v 11-14, 23-28. How is the work of the Old Testament priests a picture of the greater work of our priest, the Lord Jesus?

- v 11, 24: The tabernacle is a picture of the "more perfect tabernacle" outside creation—the place of God's ultimate, full presence: heaven.
- v 12-14: Christ did not enter this heavenly tabernacle through sacrificing an animal, but "by his own blood". His sacrifice completely "cleans" us.
- v 24-27: The priests kept having to offer sacrifices (both for themselves and for the people); Christ, as our priest, has offered a sacrifice, but it is "once for all", "to take away the sins of many" (v 26, 27).

So Christ is our priest, just like the Old Testament priests. But his work is in the heavenly tabernacle, and he has offered a sacrifice—himself—that is sufficient to completely clean us of our sins, for ever. He now stands in God's presence in the heavenly tabernacle—and so we stand there with him too (just as Israel was brought into God's presence by the priest).

8. How are these verses [Exodus 40 v 34-38] a fitting end to the book as a whole, and to the chapters detailing the design and building of the tabernacle?

The book ends with "the glory of the LORD [filling] the tabernacle" (v 34, 35). From now on, God's people will live with the presence of God among them (v 37-38—until Ezekiel

10, centuries later).

This glory is the climax of the construction of the tabernacle; and it's the climax of the story of the exodus. God has rescued his people from slavery and death so that they can enjoy his presence and see his glory. Everything so far has been leading up to this moment. Of all the blessings God gives (and there are many), this is the greatest: God himself, in his glory.

- **What is the only problem with the presence of the cloud of glory (v 35)?** No one can stand in it—even Moses! God's glory is something that even the greatest of Israelites, and of humanity, cannot dwell in.

9. Read Luke 9 v 28-36. What are the links between the events of Exodus 40 at Mount Sinai and the events recorded by Luke on this mountain? (It may help you to know that "departure" in v 31 is literally "exodus", and "shelters" in v 33 is literally "tabernacles".)

- Moses is an important figure in both.
- Moses, through whom God performed the first "exodus", discusses with Jesus how he will achieve the ultimate "exodus" when he reaches Jerusalem.
- Peter suggests they build "tabernacles"—but he has missed the point, because the true tabernacle, the presence of God in Jesus his Son, is already there.
- As in Exodus 40, the cloud of God's presence comes down upon them.
- As he did at Sinai, God speaks from the cloud.

- **Where is God's glory to be found, according to God (v 34-36)?** In Jesus. Moses, Elijah and the cloud do not stay around: but Jesus does. The message from heaven is: Jesus. He is the place where God's glory is seen and experienced.

10. Read Ephesians 2 v 21-22. How does Paul link the Old Testament tabernacle/temple with the New Testament church?
Paul is talking about the church, where Jew and Gentile are united in Christ. And he is saying that the place where people can meet God is no longer the tabernacle, nor the temple that replaced it. Your church is now the place where people meet God as you proclaim and live the gospel.

Encourage your group to look back at Q4 and see what the church is, based on what the tabernacle was:

- Like the ark, we are the place where God reigns.
- Like the table, we are the place God eats with his people in the communion meal.
- Like the lampstand, we are the place from which the light of the gospel shines.
- Like the lampstand, we are the place people can find guidance and clarity.
- Like the law, we are the place where creation is being re-ordered.
- Like the priest, we can enter God's holy presence.

- **If God's address in the Old Testament was "The Tabernacle, Sinai wilderness" and then "The Temple, Jerusalem", what is it now? Why is this exciting and challenging?** God's address is now "Your Church, Your Town". The tabernacle was once the model of God's home; now the church is. Your local church is the place in your locality where God has decided to dwell, and to reveal his glory—and we all get to be a part of that! This should cause us to feel more excited about and committed to our local church body—but it is also challenging. How fitting a home for God's glory are we? Are there ways in which we are unmoved by God's glory or unconcerned about displaying God's glory?

- **Read 1 Corinthians 6 v 19-20. How does Paul apply tabernacle/temple language to us here?** Paul goes even further here, because he says that individual Christians—you and I—are temples of the Holy Spirit. Paul is inviting us to think about what we would deem appropriate and inappropriate behaviour in the temple. You might want to think about a cathedral. Whatever you think about cathedrals, they tend to make people behave with a certain reverence. The principle seems to be, If you wouldn't do it in the temple, then you shouldn't do it all—because now you are the temple, the place on earth where God dwells.

11. APPLY: How has the book of Exodus as a whole caused you to be:
- **more in awe of God?**
- **more understanding of who God is?**
- **more grateful that you are part of his people?**
- **more excited about your life, your future and your church?**

This is an opportunity to reflect on the book as a whole. If you are short of time, tell your group members to pick one or two of these four categories. Since your group will all have different answers, get them to write their own answers down before sharing them with the group.

12. APPLY: Sum up the message of this part of Israel's history in eight words.
This is not easy! But it will help your group to focus on what they see as the core of Exodus. You could put people into pairs to discuss their answer, and then share them. Do gently point it out if anyone's summary doesn't focus on God! Encourage members to memorise their eight words.

Good Book Guides
The full range

OLD TESTAMENT

Exodus: 8 Studies
Tim Chester
ISBN: 9781784980269

Judges: 6 Studies
Timothy Keller
ISBN: 9781908762887

Ruth: 4 Studies
Tim Chester
ISBN: 9781905564910

David: 6 Studies
Nathan Buttery
ISBN: 9781904889984

1 Samuel: 6 Studies
Tim Chester
ISBN: 9781909919594

2 Samuel: 6 Studies
Tim Chester
ISBN: 9781784982195

Nehemiah: 8 Studies
Eric Mason
ISBN: 9781784986773

1 Kings 1–11: 8 Studies
James Hughes
ISBN: 9781907377976

Elijah: 5 Studies
Liam Goligher
ISBN: 9781909559240

Esther: 7 Studies
Jane McNabb
ISBN: 9781908317926

Psalms: 6 Studies
Tim Chester
ISBN: 9781904889960

Psalms: 7 Studies
Christopher Ash & Alison Mitchell
ISBN: 9781784984182

Proverbs: 8 Studies
Kathleen Nielson & Rachel Jones
ISBN: 9781784984304

Iaaiah: 8 Studies
Tim Chester
ISBN: 9781784985608

Ezekiel: 6 Studies
Tim Chester
ISBN: 9781904889274

Daniel: 7 Studies
David Helm
ISBN: 9781910307328

Hosea: 8 Studies
Dan Wells
ISBN: 9781905564255

Jonah: 6 Studies
Stephen Witmer
ISBN: 9781907377433

Micah: 6 Studies
Stephen Um
ISBN: 9781909559738

Zechariah: 6 Studies
Tim Chester
ISBN: 9781904889267

NEW TESTAMENT

Mark: 10 Studies
Jason Meyer
ISBN: 9781784983031

Mark 1–8: 10 Studies
Tim Chester
ISBN: 9781904889281

Mark 9–16: 7 Studies
Tim Chester
ISBN: 9781904889519

Luke 1–12: 8 Studies
Mike McKinley
ISBN: 9781784980160

Luke 12–24: 8 Studies
Mike McKinley
ISBN: 9781784981174

Luke 22–24: 6 Studies
Mike McKinley
ISBN: 9781909559165

John: 7 Studies
Tim Chester
ISBN: 9781907377129

John 1-12: 8 Studies
Josh Moody
ISBN: 9781784982188

John 13-21: 8 Studies
Josh Moody
ISBN: 9781784983611

Acts 1-12: 8 Studies
R. Albert Mohler
ISBN: 9781910307007

Acts 13-28: 8 Studies
R. Albert Mohler
ISBN: 9781910307014

Romans 1–7: 7 Studies
Timothy Keller
ISBN: 9781908762924

Romans 8–16: 7 Studies
Timothy Keller
ISBN: 9781910307311

1 Corinthians 1–9:
7 Studies
Mark Dever
ISBN: 9781908317681

1 Corinthians 10–16:
8 Studies
Mark Dever & Carl Laferton
ISBN: 9781908317964

1 Corinthians:
8 Studies
Andrew Wilson
ISBN: 9781784986254

2 Corinthians:
7 Studies
Gary Millar
ISBN: 9781784983895

Galatians: 7 Studies
Timothy Keller
ISBN: 9781908762566

Ephesians: 10 Studies
Thabiti Anyabwile
ISBN: 9781907377099

Ephesians: 8 Studies
Richard Coekin
ISBN: 9781910307694

Philippians: 7 Studies
Steven J. Lawson
ISBN: 9781784981181

Colossians: 6 Studies
Mark Meynell
ISBN: 9781906334246

1 Thessalonians:
7 Studies
Mark Wallace
ISBN: 9781904889533

1&2 Timothy: 7 Studies
Phillip Jensen
ISBN: 9781784980191

Titus: 5 Studies
Tim Chester
ISBN: 9781909919631

Hebrews: 8 Studies
Michael J. Kruger
ISBN: 9781784986049

James: 6 Studies
Sam Allberry
ISBN: 9781910307816

1 Peter: 6 Studies
Juan R. Sanchez
ISBN: 9781784980177

2 Peter & Jude: 6 Studies
Miguel Núñez
ISBN: 9781784987121

1 John: 7 Studies
Nathan Buttery
ISBN: 9781904889953

Revelation: 7 Studies
Tim Chester
ISBN: 9781910307021

TOPICAL

Man of God: 10 Studies
Anthony Bewes & Sam Allberry
ISBN: 9781904889977

Biblical Womanhood:
10 Studies
Sarah Collins
ISBN: 9781907377532

The Apostles' Creed:
10 Studies
Tim Chester
ISBN: 9781905564415

Promises Kept: Bible Overview: 9 Studies
Carl Laferton
ISBN: 9781908317933

The Reformation Solas
6 Studies
Jason Helopoulos
ISBN: 9781784981501

Contentment: 6 Studies
Anne Woodcock
ISBN: 9781905564668

Women of Faith:
8 Studies
Mary Davis
ISBN: 9781904889526

Meeting Jesus: 8 Studies
Jenna Kavonic
ISBN: 9781905564460

Heaven: 6 Studies
Andy Telfer
ISBN: 9781909919457

Making Work Work:
8 Studies
Marcus Nodder
ISBN: 9781908762894

The Holy Spirit: 8 Studies
Pete & Anne Woodcock
ISBN: 9781905564217

Experiencing God:
6 Studies
Tim Chester
ISBN: 9781906334437

Real Prayer: 7 Studies
Anne Woodcock
ISBN: 9781910307595

Mission: 7 Studies
Alan Purser
ISBN: 9781784983628

Church: 8 Studies
Anne Woodcock
ISBN: 9781784984199

Talking to Our Father:
7 Studies
Tim Chester
ISBN: 9781784985202

thegoodbook

COMPANY

BIBLICAL | RELEVANT | ACCESSIBLE

At The Good Book Company, we are dedicated to helping Christians and local churches grow. We believe that God's growth process always starts with hearing clearly what he has said to us through his timeless word—the Bible.

Ever since we opened our doors in 1991, we have been striving to produce Bible-based resources that bring glory to God. We have grown to become an international provider of user-friendly resources to the Christian community, with believers of all backgrounds and denominations using our books, Bible studies, devotionals, evangelistic resources, and DVD-based courses.

We want to equip ordinary Christians to live for Christ day by day, and churches to grow in their knowledge of God, their love for one another, and the effectiveness of their outreach.

Call us for a discussion of your needs or visit one of our local websites for more information on the resources and services we provide.

Your friends at The Good Book Company

thegoodbook.com | thegoodbook.co.uk
thegoodbook.com.au | thegoodbook.co.nz
thegoodbook.co.in